An Old House

in

Greenville, Virginia

AN OLD HOUSE

IN

GREENVILLE, VIRGINIA

❦

A STUDY OF HUMAN INTENTION

IN

VERNACULAR ARCHITECTURE

Michael S. Shutty, Jr.

The McDonald & Woodward Publishing Company
Blacksburg, Virginia
1997

The McDonald & Woodward Publishing Company
P. O. Box 10308, Blacksburg, Virginia 24062–0308

**An Old House in Greenville, Virginia
A Study of Human Intention in Vernacular
Architecture**

© 1996 by The McDonald & Woodward Publishing Company

Composition by Rowan Mountain, Inc., Blacksburg, Virginia

Printed in the United States of America by McNaughton & Gunn, Inc., Saline, Michigan

02 01 00 99 98 97   10 9 8 7 6 5 4 3 2 1

First printing February 1997

Library of Congress Cataloging-in-Publication Data
Shutty, Michael S., 1957–
    An old house in Greenville, Virginia : a study of human intention
in vernacular architecture / Michael S. Shutty, Jr.
        p.   cm.
    Includes bibliographical references and index.
    ISBN 0-939923-66-1 (alk. paper)
    1. Robert Steele House (Greenville, Augusta County, Va.)
    2. Architecture, Domestic—Virginia—Greenville, Augusta County)
    3. Vernacular architecture—Virginia—Greenville (Augusta County)
    4. Greenville (Augusta County, Va.)—Buildings structures, etc.
    I. Title.
    NA7238.G69S56   1996   96-41855
    728'.372'09755916—dc20   CIP

Contents

Acknowledgments

Many people have helped me along the way. My wife, Dana, not only survived those "long book weekends" but also tolerated the many walks around Greenville to see everything "one more time." Her support and editorial keenness is evident in both the tone (and grammar) found in my writing. I want to thank John Brake, Berl and Edna Steele and Dr. Hansford Thomas Jr. for sharing their experiences; I have been inspired by their pride in Greenville. A number of folks invited me into their homes including Velma Spitler, Mark Amis and Kathleen Vance, Laurence and Karen Reed, Mike and Sharon Dahlin, Charlie and Virginia Brown, Keith and Naomi Grove and Mr. and Mrs. Price. Richard Hamrick and David Schwartz very generously provided some great old photographs from their collections. Also, John Davis and his staff were extremely helpful in guiding me through the Augusta County Court Records; I extend the same thanks to the Staunton City Courthouse staff. Local librarians from Augusta County, Staunton and Waynesboro also shared their time with me for which I am grateful. The Virginia State Library and the Virginia Historical Landmarks Commission provided information as well. Earlier versions of the manuscript were read by Mrs. William Bushman, Dr. Kenneth Brasfield and John Williamson. Patricia Higgins helped me figure out how to manage my house history business. Jennifer Francis did the index. To all of you I am indebted.

Credits

All photographs, maps, and drawings are credited to the author with the following exceptions: Figure 11: (drawing) Mutual Insurance records, VHLC; Figure 14: Augusta County court records; Figure 15: Augusta County court records; Figure 16: Augusta County court records; Figure 26: Augusta County court records; Figure 27: Richard M. and Thomas B. Hamrick Collection, Staunton, Virginia; Figure 28: (top photograph only) Richard M. and Thomas B. Hamrick Collection, Staunton, Virginia; Figure 29: J. Hotchkiss and J. A. Waddell, 1885; Figure 30: Richard M. and Thomas B. Hamrick Collection, Staunton, Virginia; Figure 32: Richard M. and Thomas B. Hamrick Collection, Staunton, Virginia; Figure 33: (bottom photograph only) Richard M. and Thomas B. Hamrick Collection, Staunton, Virginia; Figure 34: Historical resources survey, Augusta County, VHLC; Figure 35: Camera and Palette Collection, Staunton, Virginia.

Prologue

The Robert Steele House is a modest dwelling whose history is intertwined with the social and economic growth of a small village named Greenville located in the Valley of Virginia. With the old north-south Valley Turnpike as its Main Street, Greenville was once a thriving marketplace and busy stage-coach stop located between Staunton and Lexington. In the late 1880s, the town reached its zenith, boasting two railroad lines, several mills, and a choice of fine hotels for its visitors.

The Robert Steele House fronts on Main Street and represents an early example of the vernacular brick structures which were once symbolic of American prosperity in the Valley. Soon after it was built, a center-hall floor plan was added; this modification marked the beginning of an era when the house transcended purely functional demands and became a center for social and leisure activity. This was an era when the Valley was evolving from its "backwoods" beginning to an established network of rural communities. Since its construction in 1829, the Robert Steele House has stood as a Greenville landmark throughout most of the town's two-hundred year history.

A wide range of people called the Robert Steele House their home. Robert Steele himself was a prominent farmer and entrepreneur. The house was later inhabited by father and son saddle-makers who designed and marketed their own patented "saddle-seat." Other owners included merchants, real estate speculators, and two physicians — one of whom was a key witness testifying on Cyrus McCormick's behalf when his 1831 patent for the "reaper" was challenged. A Civil War veteran who served under Stonewall Jackson and later founded a summer resort in the Blue Ridge Mountains was one of its eccentric residents.

This is a chronicle of the many influences that shaped the building and evolution of the Robert Steele House. It is also a history of Augusta County, Greenville, and some of its people.

1

Discovery

To become intimately acquainted with an old house and to attempt to "know it" is a highly personal endeavor. Few objects in our lives are as dear to us as our homes. Our most personal moments — with family, friends, and ourselves — have taken place under their protective roofs. Old houses in particular possess an allure that cuts deeply into our consciousness. Indeed, it is an eerie yet exhilarating experience to explore the intimate spaces within an old, long-vacant family home. This feeling can be particularly acute when the motions of past lives present themselves in a well-worn floor or in the discovery of personal objects left behind.

Old houses always evoke strong emotions in us, as they have withstood the passage of time, immortal against the ever-changing human landscape. That weather-beaten farmstead silhouetted against the hill just outside of town represents a cultural archetype in America. Much more than just an empty shell, it stands as a monument to those who came before us. It is a repository of lives passed, preserved in a unique juxtaposition of brick, wood and glass. Evolving with their owners, old houses are a testament to all who lived there.

When I first discovered the old house for sale in Greenville, I was lured by its plain and unpretentious facade. It stood tall and narrow, flanked by two chimneys. The handmade brick had weathered to a red and orange mosaic speckled with traces of blue-black glazing. Brick headers alternated with stretchers in a decorative fashion, capped with a delicately curved cornice of molded bricks. The roof pitch was precipitous with the two chimneys extending boldly out from the walls and reaching nearly four feet above the ridge, like pillars lending stability to an already stout structure. The walls were sixteen inches thick! Overall, the look was clearly of a bygone era. . . . Yes, the house was quite ancient looking.

   This aesthetic awakened a deep-felt sense of adventure in me, as I imagined all that this house had witnessed. The very idea that the building before me had survived generation after generation was overwhelming. How could anyone discard a structure of this significance?

Figure 1. Robert Steele House, circa 1829. A tall narrow profile with gable end chimneys and minimal adornments on the facade are characteristics of the antebellum Virginia Valley house. The structure abuts Greenville's Main Street, consistent with the custom of the early nineteenth century; such siting allowed easy road access during bitter weather and did not waste yard space. The building originally had a second front door under the left second floor window and was without a porch. The lateral frame section to the right was added sometime between 1841 and 1856, whereas the rear addition was built after 1902.

The realtor groaned when I inquired about its condition. After all, there were many more habitable prospects on the market. Upon inspection, decades of neglect and defamation were obvious. Yet its dignity was preserved in its form. Large, decorative mantels and thick moldings dominated the front rooms. A single bead sufficed as the predominant motif — simple, yet to my eye, understated elegance. The floors were of heart pine, gently scalloped by wear. . . .

I submitted a contract that day, packed up my belongings, and moved into the Greenville house the following spring.

2
Material Culture

I was surprised and disappointed when I discovered that architectural writers had largely ignored houses like mine. Accounts of modest houses were eclipsed by those of the aristocracy. At the local library, I found an entire shelf of glossy, oversized pictorial books depicting very early, very large or very famous houses — all of them listed in the National Register of Historical Places. Even the dryly academic architectural field guides relied on descriptions of large mansions to illustrate period details. Several recently published guidebooks did include sections on "folk" or "vernacular houses," but meager text accompanied the pictures.

Although it did not resemble the opulent nineteenth century homes celebrated in the library texts, I was convinced that the Greenville house was historically significant. Despite having only two floors and four rooms, the detailing revealed a deliberate attention to style. The mantels and moldings went beyond function; they were meant to seduce the eye no matter how many times one entered the room. Certainly, it was a *grand* house when it was built in 1829, for it was constructed of brick and located prominently along Main Street.

The house had not been completely ignored by historians, however, as it was included in a county-wide survey of nineteenth century houses conducted by Ann McCleary under the auspices of the Virginia Historical Landmarks Commission (VHLC). The survey for Augusta County was completed in 1982 and included architectural analyses, photographic records, title searches, and oral histories for all ante-bellum structures. A brief narrative was completed on each structure and cataloged at the VHLC offices in Richmond, Virginia. No less than one-hundred-sixty of these houses were similar in design to the one in Greenville.

I was reassured to discover that a growing number of scholars are choosing "typical" houses as legitimate subjects for intensive research. In fact, these scholars are leaving their university offices and taking field-trips to rummage through old houses. Like forensic detectives, they examine every detail —from minute paint chips to nail hole patterns — to figure out how the rooms were laid out, altered, and expanded over time. I originally thought this kind of detail work was re-served for the likes of Jefferson's Monticello.

Dressed in blue-jeans, they call themselves social and architectural historians, cultural geographers, archaeologists and preservationists. Together, this alliance of academics is defining the field of Vernacular Architecture. It is a young field, still experiencing an identity crisis, as no one is sure how to define its boundaries which for the traditionalist includes "the old, the rural and the domestic" but for others may include any typical building. Certainly, the Greenville house would have merit in their eyes.

These scholars argue that the understanding of everyday life in early America would be incomplete without a study of the relics left behind by the masses. They call these relics "material culture" of which houses are a part. The importance of examining these relics appears obvious, yet the American history we all learned in grade school has been largely de-rived from written records, paintings and objects of the upper classes. Our history is portrayed as the activities of famous people punctuated by major political events occurring along a timeline. Little attention is given to the day-to-day experi-ences of the common folk — men and women like most of us.

Just as today's media has ignored the plight of the com-mon man while becoming obsessed with the antics of Wash-ington politicians, so too has the history of everyday life in America been neglected in comparison with the studied life of a president or general. One reason for this neglect is that the privileged classes left many more records for researchers to study. They owned more land, conducted more business, had more leisure time to keep a diary or sit for a portrait, and were more interesting to the biographers of the period. In contrast, common folks owned little land and conducted only mundane business. They often could not write and had little time to sit for pictures. It comes as no surprise that few biographers were interested in them. Yet, their lives were full! They were busy settling a new frontier, forging a living from the land, and building houses. So instead of writings, we have their tools, their belongings, and their houses.

This point has been powerfully stated by vernacular researchers Dell Upton and John Vlach:

The study of vernacular architecture is fundamentally a humanistic study. We appreciate buildings and landscapes and furniture as handsome objects, but if we really understand them we know that what is most important is to appreciate the people who made them. The study of intention becomes the ultimate one in vernacular architecture studies, because it is the study of people acting. It shows us people in charge of their own lives, people engaged with their surrounds in a critical way, people making their own histories in the face of authorities trying to make it for them.

A typical house reveals much about its builders and residents. It provides insights into the rhythms of everyday life in the local community. It reveals clues about larger economic and cultural trends, not to mention advances in construction methods and materials. As such, an old house can serve as a focal point around which an original and broadly defined historical sketch can be organized. Although most researchers use survey methods to highlight common features shared among many houses, it is my intent to examine one house in magnified-glass detail.

Too often house histories are presented as a series of isolated conveyances occurring along a timeline. Lists of successive house owners (i.e., title chains) are without depth unless interpreted along with an appreciation of changing economic fortunes, war, social fashions, acculturation, and the like. Together, these events reveal a story. To truly know a house is to piece together its story like a jigsaw puzzle where the shape and shading of each piece must be considered. Indeed, the search is rewarded many times over with the exhilaration one feels when old documents are discovered or bits of information bring forth new understanding — this interpretive process is truly *history in the making.*

3

The Quest Begins

My quest began in the lounging chair. Amidst stacks of readily accessible history texts detailing the early settlement of the Valley of Virginia, I sat hoping to trace the development of Greenville. Many of these books were published in the mid-to-late nineteenth century and included oral histories passed down from the original settlers. Unfortunately, most Valley histories were painted with a broad brush and included barely a mention of Greenville. For example, in his *History of Augusta County* published in 1882, Lewis Peyton devoted but four sentences exclusively to Greenville. Joseph Waddell did no better in his *Annals of Augusta County* published in 1886. And a more recent text by Richard MacMaster entitled *Augusta County History: 1865–1950* ignored Greenville almost entirely, excepting an early-1900s photo of its Main Street. This is not to say that these works were trivial or unhelpful; to the contrary, they provided invaluable insights for understanding Greenville's development — but precious little has been written about the town itself.

Fortunately, there was some Greenville history to be found in a few short *Staunton News Leader* pieces scattered across several decades. Of particular note was the weekly column entitled "Shenandoah Sketches" written by Joe Nutt featuring historic sites throughout Augusta County. In addition, Greenville's local historian, John Brake, wrote a brief article in the Fall, 1981, *Augusta County Historical Society Bulletin*. In reading these articles, it became apparent that the same information was repeated over and over, suggesting that very little original research existed. Greenville is not alone however; many small towns in the Virginia Valley are similarly "undiscovered." It is of note that Brake has just finished a book detailing the genealogy of the town's families entitled, *The History of Greenville, Virginia*. This magnum opus is destined to become a much sought after reference — Greenville will be forever indebted to Brake.

So the armchair research was short-lived. The next step was a title search using *Deed Book* records in the Augusta County courthouse. This task began by using *Grantor/Grantee* indices to trace property titles backwards in time. Information gleaned from deeds included names of owners and their spouses, dates of ownership, prices paid, and property descriptions which only rarely mentioned houses or other buildings.

This line of inquiry was also short-lived; an unrecorded deed brought my title-chain to an abrupt halt in the year 1841. Using the names on the *Land Tax* records, most of the missing deeds were found. But some deeds were never found, underscoring the reality that court records are often incomplete — and this state of affairs worsens the farther back in time one goes. Fortunately, Augusta County records are among the most complete in Virginia.

The *Land Tax* records provided owners names and estimates of land and building values for every lot in Greenville from 1800 to the present. This information facilitated quick access to other deeds, and together these sources provided valuable clues about building activity, economic development, and prominent landlords in town. A picture of Greenville was beginning to emerge which heretofore had never been seen!

But other questions arose: who were these people and what kind of lives did they lead? The next step was to examine records of life's milestones: *Birth, Marriage, and Death* registers. Unfortunately, these records are notoriously incomplete before 1850. Some of these gaps have been remedied by previous researchers who have studied other sources, compiling their findings in user-friendly indices. For example, a book entitled *Here Lyeth* by Dorothy Weaver included names and gravestone dates for many local cemeteries in Augusta County. These records, albeit incomplete, provided ages of some house owners and their families and facilitated interpretations about maturity, stage of life struggles, and the like. Due to the continuous movement of many early Augusta County families, I searched many of the aforementioned records for Rockingham and Rockbridge Counties as well. It would not have been unreasonable to scan Tennessee, Kentucky, Ohio, and Missouri records too.

Probably the most colorful sources of information about the families who lived in Greenville were the *Will Book* records and *Chancery Court* records. In addition to wills, these records included letters of administration, and occasionally, complete inventories of personal property. Chancery Court records often included letters penned by family members themselves. This collection of records was indexed by year/ name and stored in numbered, metal boxes located in a far corner of the Augusta County courthouse. Documents for each court case were housed in a thick paper wrapping, bound together by a small string.

Searching the *Will Book* and *Chancery Court* records required considerable sleuthing, as the records were often incomplete, cryptic, and sometimes recorded in a name not previously encountered (for example, when a female heir initiated a chancery suit under her married name). Some estates were not settled for many years following a person's death, particularly if a distant relative initiated the chancery process. Many times records simply were not kept, especially for common folk who may not have recorded a will and whose property was quietly divided-up among surviving family members. In fact, this latter scenario would be more often the case were it not that many folks owed money to local merchants prompting a legally-supervised estate settlement.

In addition to the records reviewed above, there were many sources of historical information about specific events such as *United States Census* records, Military records, Church records, and *Order Book* records (i.e., civil/criminal court records) to name but a few. Genealogists have their own immense network of magazines and books too numerous to list — I was amazed at how many researchers make a living by organizing and reorganizing all of these records!

Old newspapers (mostly from Staunton) often reported local news in the form of letters to the editor, telling about Greenville events. Greenville even had its own Wednesday weekly named *The Greenville Banner*, published by J. B. Burwell between 1882 and 1885. The first volume is housed in the Virginia State Archives. Burwell later moved to Staunton and published the *Augusta County Argus* wherein he regularly ran a column entitled "Greenville Gleanings." He obviously enjoyed fashioning alliterative headings — others for the area included "Middlebrook Matters" and "Waynesboro Whisperings."

Relics and old photos, when they could be found, provided information unobtainable elsewhere. Photos, in particular, revealed the character of the place: the condition of its streets, the uses made of its buildings, the expressions of its people.

Ledger books, letters, diaries, and letterheads all contributed to the social, economic, and cultural interpretations of day-to-day life in early Greenville. These items must be discovered, as they typically reside in private collections. Some historic materials about Greenville have surfaced in local estate auctions, but this is becoming less common. Once while attending a paper auction, my curiosity was captured by a tattered journal, nearly deteriorated beyond legibility. It shared the table with several uncatalogued books, most of them first and second editions of history texts dating between 1880 and 1940. Upon inspection, I recognized many of the names recorded and discovered it to be an account book from a wagoner and tannery operator in Greenville with entries dating from 1849 well into the Civil War!

Finally, oral histories from old-time Greenville residents have been invaluable. I audiotaped interviews and used old photos to stimulate memories. These reminiscences revealed much about the person's own culture and feelings, which too, are part of the town's heritage.

I sometimes encountered barriers that I did not know existed, but I rarely met with anyone who was unfriendly or unwilling to talk about their town. Once, upon first meeting an elderly woman who had been born in the Greenville house, I was sharply informed that she did not approve of my having painted the framed house additions to match the brick. "The house was always white for as long as I can remember," she said. Despite our apparent disagreement, the conversation continued as she shared her recollections. As I turned to leave, she added — still making clear her hesitation in saying so — that perhaps she "might get used to that new color one day."

In the telling of their stories, these people invited me to share their pride in, and obvious affection for, the town of Greenville.

4

Back to the Beginning

Historians of the Valley of Virginia have traditionally started their accounts by tracing the Scotch-Irish and Pennsylvania Germans back to their Old World beginnings. At first, I found myself skipping these early chapters; I was not interested in Ireland or Germany, and wanted a more circumscribed history. But early Valley history is a story of people searching for a better life. I soon realized that the evolution of Greenville, and the context in which to understand the house, can only be appreciated by considering the *Zeitgeist* — "the spirit of the times" — which lured these thousands of settlers into the Valley of Virginia.

Before the arrival of European settlers, the Valley was inhabited by many nomadic Indian tribes who relied upon hunting and fishing, and to a lesser extent small-scale farming, for their livelihood. In contrast to the oft-sketched pastoral images of native American life, there were frequent clashes over hunting rights. The Delawares and the Catawbas, for example, fought violently throughout the Valley during the early 1730s. Peyton noted that such wars were a "constant occurrence." It was the Shawnees however, described as fierce, restless, and contemptuous, who were the most feared in the region. Always on the move, they invited conflicts with others and were certainly wary of newcomers. It was during these turbulent times that the earliest European pioneers were arriving in the northern part of the Valley of Virginia and forming their opinions about the Indians.

Of importance to the eventual settlement of the Valley, and Greenville in particular, were the Indian paths traversing the countryside in many directions. The most prominent path ran north-south through the center of the Valley from its northern-most point near Winchester, Virginia, to Bristol, Tennessee. This path meandered widely to reduce the steep grades in the otherwise rolling and rock-studded Valley plain. Initially called the "Indian Road," this path later became a major corridor for European settlers and soon was known as the "Great Wagon Road" or just "Great Road."

As early as 1745, this road was officially recognized by the colonial government as a public road and exists today as US Route 11. Over the years, many of the twists and turns have been straightened so that very little of the original roadway remains. Many times I find myself engaging in the Sunday-driver's pursuit of searching for the over-grown vestiges of these abandoned twists and turns while traveling along US Route 11. The bypassed Main Streets of Burketown, Mint Spring and Greenville are but some of the results of this straightening.

In his *History of the Shenandoah Valley*, William Couper provides the most thorough description of the original road, noting that its present location in Greenville is unchanged; it is likely that this site offered a natural fording of the South River. In contrast, it is surprising to find that large portions of the original road were located a mile or more east of US Route 11. For example, upon entering Rockingham County, the Great Road ran along the base of Massanutten through Keezletown and Weyers Cave and continued via Cross Keys and New Hope to the Old Tinkling Springs Road just south of Fishersville. Some have suggested that it was George Washington who, in the 1750s, was responsible for surveying parts of the new road running west of Keezletown through Harrisonburg. This is a somewhat romantic notion which is probably why the story has persisted for so long. Nevertheless, it is important to recognize that several alternate roads existed, all about the same time. Hence, there was not *one*

Great Road in the 1750s.

Throughout the late 1600s, English colonists ventured deeper west from the Tidewater area to explore the frontier bordering the Blue Ridge Mountains. It was not until August 1716 that Colonel Alexander Spotswood, then Governor of Virginia, and his fifty "Knights of the Golden Horseshoe" crested the Blue Ridge at Swift Run Gap (where US Route 33 now crosses) and gazed upon the Valley. What they saw was an uninhabited landscape of rolling hills and thick forests divided by the three forks of the Shenandoah River. Although a German explorer named John Lederer is credited with first entering the southern part of the Virginia Valley between 1669 and 1670, it was Spotswood's expedition that gained the wider audience and found its way into the history books.

As was the imperialistic fashion, Spotswood claimed the Valley and all lands beyond for King George I of England. Upon returning to the colonial capital at Williamsburg, Spotswood popularized the Valley, depicting the land as a paradise, free of savages, fertile, and rich with game. The newly discovered frontier became part of Essex County which, when divided, became part of Spotsylvania County, and later part of Orange County in 1734.

In contrast to Spotswood's chosen path over the Blue Ridge, the first settlers to build their homes in this wilderness did not cross the mountains from the Tidewater and Pied-mont areas. Rather, Scotch-Irish and German settlers ventured into the Valley from the north via Pennsylvania. These settlers traveled on the Great Road, which at that time was merely a narrow path. Consequently, the Valley was *not* initially settled by the English, whose migration from eastern Virginia was limited by the hardships imposed in crossing the Blue Ridge Mountains. The route taken by these pioneers traveling south from Pennsylvania is referred to as going "up" the Valley (i.e., up in elevation) toward the headwaters of the Shenandoah River. The three forks of the Shenandoah River flow northward to the confluence with the Potomac River at Harpers Ferry. Hence, the southern part of the Valley, where Greenville is located, is known as the upper Valley.

One of the earliest settlements in the Valley was established by Adam Miller (Müller) in the late 1720s near "Massanutting." Other pioneers included John Mackey, a Scotch-Irishman who settled along Timber Ridge between Steeles Tavern and Lexington in 1727, and James Kerr, who settled as early as 1730 near New Hope. This influx of migrants from the north increased throughout the 1730s. Among the newcomers was the celebrated John Lewis who traveled from Lancaster, Pennsylvania to a place near Staunton in the summer of 1732 and established a homestead called Bellfonte.

Lewis and others who soon followed him to the Augusta County region were primarily Presbyterian dissenters from the Church of England. They were called "Scotch-Irish" as most were from families who shared a Scottish ancestry but lived in Ulster or Northern Ireland. Since Greenville was primarily a Scotch-Irish settlement, it is important to examine their background and how it shaped their character.

The term "Scotch-Irish" is a misnomer, as it refers to the Scottish lowlanders who emigrated to Northern Ireland in the early 1600s. Scotland was mired in the dark ages throughout the seventeenth century, governed haphazardly by feudal lords. Life for the tenant farmer was hard, unpredictable, and offered almost no hope of improvement. Beginning in 1609, the English Crown (starting with James I) offered relatively inexpensive land leases in Ulster to any of the lowland Scots who wished to emigrate. This colonization was an attempt to subdue the long-standing conflict between the Roman Catholic Irish and the Protestant English. As a result, many thousands of Scots crossed the 30-mile channel to Ulster seeking economic opportunity. A second, but somewhat less compelling, reason to emigrate was to pursue religious freedom, as the Scotch Presbyterians were persecuted by the English Episcopacy.

Despite the hardships of establishing new homes on the Ulster frontier, the Scots flourished for a time. The character of these pioneers was shaped by this experience: men began to view themselves as free agents, not bound to social status by kinship but able to achieve an increased income and enjoy the improvement in social status it could bring. In addition to these capitalist urgings, the Ulster Scots adhered to a strict, dogmatic Presbyterianism, shaped by the rigors of carving out a life on the frontier, particularly in a land dominated by the Catholic Irish. In his tracing of the social history of the Scotch-Irish, historian James Leyburn succinctly portrayed them as rugged individualists who placed high value upon religious faith and were driven by a desire for a better life.

As a matter of curiosity, it has been noted by several historians that the Ulster Scots had little concern for domestic cleanliness. Their houses were frequently built adjacent to barns, and smaller farm animals were often sheltered from bitter weather in the house itself. Communal living, including sharing of beds and eating utensils, was the norm. Baths were said to be uncommon. These observations gave rise to the English impression that the Ulster Scots were uniformly "disgusting." Perhaps these characteristics stemmed from their long heritage as feudal serfs in Scotland where few tenants owned anything at all. Perhaps also, the English impression of the Ulster Scots was biased.

By 1717, economic and religious hardships again prompted the Ulster Scots to migrate for a second time — this time to America. English landlords began raising lease prices (called "rack-renting" or just "racking") to levels that made it difficult for farmers to make a profit. In addition, conflicts between the Church of England and the Ulster Scot's Presbyterianism intensified. These insults, coupled with multiple years of famine, launched a series of emigrations to the New World. Although more accurately called Ulster Scots, the term Scotch-Irish has been typically used to describe this group of American settlers.

The deteriorating situation in Ireland was characterized in the *Pennsylvania Gazette* on November 20, 1729, as follows:

> *The English papers have of late been frequent in their Accounts of the unhappy Circumstances of the Common People of Ireland; That Poverty, Wretchedness, Misery and Want are becoming almost universal among them; That . . . there is not Corn enough rais'd for their Subsistence one Year with another; and at the same Time the Trade and Manufactures of*

the Nation being cramp'd and discourag'd, the labouring People have little to do, and consequently are not able to purchase Bread at its present dear Rate: That the Taxes are nevertheless exceeding heavy, and Money very scarce; and add to this, that their griping, avaricious Landlords exercise over them the most merciless Racking Tyranny and Oppression. Hence it is that such Swarms of them are driven over into America.

Despite the growing number of settlers, the colonial government in Williamsburg did not legally recognize the homesteads of Lewis and others. Rather, land grants were given to prominent speculators with the idea that this would preserve the Virginia government's control over the region while providing a protective buffer between the English Piedmont and the French and Indian settlements to the west. Consequently, 118,491 acres were granted to William Beverley from Tidewater in 1736. The tract included Bellfonte and most of the area between the Blue Ridge and the Alleghenies from Waynesboro to Greenville. The grant stipulated that if Beverley and his co-grantees:

. . . do not, within the space of three years next ensuing after the date of these presents, cultivate and improve three acres part of every fifty of the tract above mentioned, upon the estate hereby granted, shall cease and be utterly determined, and thereafter it shall and may be lawful to and for us, our heirs and successors, to grant the same lands and premises, with the appurtenances, to such other person or persons as we, our heirs and successors, shall think fit.

Given this demand for rapid development, Beverley promptly built his home, which he called his "Mill Place," near the center of the tract and immediately set out to promote the sale of his land. Since some parcels were already settled, Beverley gained a *head start* by selling the land to whomever was already there. In other instances, he sold large tracts to speculators explicitly deeding them "all houses, buildings, orchards, ways, waters, watercourses" located thereon. To recruit new settlers to the area, Beverley wrote to his partner and agent, James Patton, a ship captain responsible for bringing many Scotch-Irish immigrants to America, urging him to "import families enough to take the whole off from our hands at a reasonable price." Waddell reported that

Patton sailed to Ireland twenty-five times to bring settlers to the Valley; other historians have argued that Patton acted as a recruiting agent only and did not actually captain the ships.

Similar *conditional* land grants were awarded throughout the Valley within a short period of time. Among them was 92,100 acres bordering the southern boundaries of Beverley's tract, encompassing all of Rockbridge County, which was given to Benjamin Borden in November, 1739. Like Beverley, Borden was required to entice immigrants to make their home in the Valley; in his case, one-thousand acres were awarded him for every family that "settled" on his land. As a result of the land granting process, the Valley was not settled in a progressive fashion; rather, many hundreds of homesteads were established in several regions at once. The entire Valley was populated within several years.

The prevalence of land speculation has been underestimated by many historians. A little bit of business sense could go a long way on the frontier, as land was a desirable commodity. Many profiteers followed the flow of settlers westward, buying cheap land and selling it off in smaller parcels as they went. With an annual average of two-thousand settlers passing through the Valley between 1740 and 1750, the market was ripe for rampant exploitation of land. In particular, mill sites and commercial development of towns spelled big profits for the entrepreneurial-minded.

Attracting settlers was easily done, as they were eager for the opportunities promised in this new land. Beverley sold large tracts of land for less than a shilling per acre until 1750, whereas similar land was bringing twenty shillings in Lancaster, Pennsylvania, throughout the 1740s. Furthermore, the Scotch-Irish were disliked in the northern colony; their mass exodus from Ulster alarmed the Pennsylvania government which feared that the English might be overwhelmed by their numbers, estimated to be twelve-thousand annually in the late 1740s. This sentiment was reflected as early as 1724 by James Logan, then secretary to the Province of Pennsylvania, who wrote that:

. . . it looks as if Ireland is to send all its inhabitants hither, for last week not less than six ships arrived . . . it is strange that they thus crowd where they are not wanted.

Consequently, the upper Valley swelled with Scotch-Irish settlers, prompting map-makers Joshua Fry and Peter Jefferson to label the region encompassed by the Beverley and Borden patents as the "Irish tract" on their 1750/1775 map of Virginia. Court records between 1775 and 1786 suggest that nearly sixty percent of Augusta County was composed of Scotch-Irish settlers as compared to twenty percent each of English and German settlers. So dominant were the Scotch-Irish, that eight of the twelve vestrymen of the first Augusta Parish were Presbyterians and not of the established Church of England. This tolerance of the dissenters by the Virginia government was not based upon any liberal doctrine, but was guided by the desire to rapidly populate the Valley thereby providing a protective region between eastern Virginia and the Indians.

Between 1738 and 1744, Beverley sold no less than 47,366 acres to ninety-four purchasers; this number of patents doubled by 1750. New construction intensified as migration into the Valley increased. By 1740, the Old Stone Church congregation was established several miles north of Bellfonte and Beverley's Mill Place with the Reverend John Craig as its Presbyterian minister. Although the first meeting house was of log construction, work on the stone church began soon after, and was completed in 1779. A second church, known as Tinkling Spring, was erected around 1741 several miles to the east, along the older but still heavily traveled portion of the Great Road. In 1746, the Reverend John Blair visited the region and established four additional Presbyterian congregations: North Mountain near Middlebrook, New Providence near Brownsburg, Timber Ridge between Lexington and Fairfield, and Forks of the James near Lexington.

During the early years, the pioneers experienced tense but peaceful relations with the Indians. This has been attributed to the small numbers of settlers who arrived at first, resulting in few conflicts over Valley resources. As was inevitable, conflicts increased as the European population grew. War with the French involving boundary disputes in the west intensified these conflicts. The 1750s marked the beginning of a decade of bloody skirmishes and wars in the far western reaches of the county, brought to a crescendo with the defeat (777 killed) of General Braddock's British/Colonial Army in the summer of 1755 along the Monogahela River in what is now West Virginia.

The last reported Indian raid within present-day Augusta County occurred in the fall of 1764 when approximately thirty Shawnees crept into the Valley on a random killing spree. The party surprised and murdered Alexander and Mary Crawford at their homestead before moving towards Churchville. Along the way, the raiders happened upon and killed John Trimble and took two hostages. A hastily formed rescue party pursued the Indians, and after a fight, freed the hostages. Trimble had the unfortunate distinction of being the last such casualty in the area.

No documented skirmishes ever occurred in the vicinity of Greenville, yet news of conflicts between roaming parties of Indians and settlers located in the nearby Allegheny Mountains contributed to a generalized fear and intolerance of Indians which lasted well into the nineteenth century. The existence of a stone fort in the area was noted in the May 29, 1888, edition of the *Augusta County Argus* as follows, "near Greenville is the old Doak stone house, used in Indian times as a fort." By the 1780s, any real Indian threat in the Valley was gone.

In November 1738, the Virginia General Assembly created Augusta and Frederick Counties from Orange County. Establishing a county government was delayed however, until "a sufficient number of inhabitants for appointing justices of the peace and other officers" could be substantiated. By 1745, Augusta County boasted a large enough population to permit the building of a courthouse and the appointment of court officers. This courthouse was indeed a meager proposition: a crude log structure measuring 18 by 38 feet located at Beverley's Mill Place. At the time, the new county government served about 1670 persons; this figure swelled to about twenty-thousand whites and one-thousand blacks over the next twenty years and more than doubled that figure by the Revolutionary War.

Among the earliest court orders were those concerned with building roads. Between March 1745 and June 1746, a series of road improvements were ordered along the "Indian

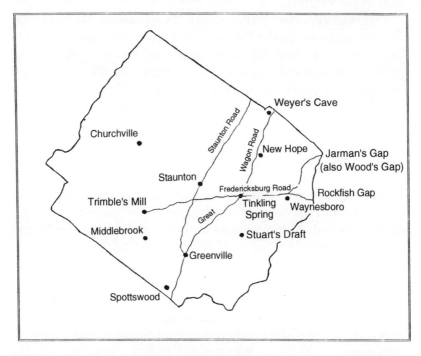

Figure 2. Old roads and gaps in the Greenville vicinity. The Great Wagon Road entered Augusta County at Weyers Cave (Virginia Route 276) and continued south to New Hope and Tinkling Spring (Virginia Route 608). The road passed west of Stuarts Draft (Virginia Route 652) and followed the path taken by US Route 340 to Greenville. The road entered Greenville along the Ridge Road (Virginia Route 657). Another early road from Staunton (Virginia Route 613) entered Greenville along the north bank of the South River (Virginia Route 1206). This road continued south, passing Spottswood, enroute to Timber Ridge. One of the earliest roads traversing the Valley in an east-west direction was the Fredericksburg Road which went from Trimble's Mill past Tinkling Spring to the Blue Ridge at Jarman's Gap. An alternative route over the mountains crossed at Rockfish Gap. Both gaps coexisted as travel routes during the mid-1700s.

Road." According to Couper, these improvements probably ran from the courthouse in Staunton to Harrisonburg, and on to Lacey Springs, where it joined the original Indian Road. In the following year, a second road was ordered by the court from Staunton, east to the Blue Ridge, and "thence to the falls of the James River and Fredericksburg." This latter road crossed the Blue Ridge at Jarman's Gap and connected to the "three-notched road" leading to Charlottesville.

In 1748, forty-four half-acre lots were laid out at the Mill Place and the town of Staunton came into being. Staunton was an immediate economic success, as trade flourished throughout the upper Valley in the 1750s. Mills and distilleries proliferated and cattle became a major export. In this regard, Philip Vickers Fithian, a Presbyterian minister who stayed in Staunton in late 1775, noted in his diary, "the people here live well" and went on to describe the plentiful meats and produce that filled dining tables across the countryside.

That there were profits to be made from establishing a town was underscored by the promotion and sale of lots in Staunton. Half-acre town lots sold for five pounds each in 1750, and by 1755, this price had doubled. Only five years later, some town lots were commanding prices of one-hundred or two-hundred pounds! Farmland valuations appeared sluggish by comparison. This potential attracted speculators from as far away as Fredericksburg. It is no wonder that an additional twenty-five acres were divided into town lots on the west side of town in 1787. By the end of the eighteenth century, land values in the Valley were among the highest in Virginia.

Augusta County initially stretched west into the Ohio territory including twenty-one present-day Virginia counties, all of Kentucky, and parts of West Virginia and Pennsylvania. It was divided several times from 1770 when Botetourt County was formed until 1790 when Bath County was formed, leaving Augusta County at its currently defined boundaries.

5

Early Building

Anyone who has visited the Museum of American Frontier Culture, located in Staunton, cannot help but be impressed with the meticulous reconstruction of actual farmsites from sixteenth and seventeenth century Germany, Ireland, and England. The exhibits are situated such that visitors are first exposed to the traditions practiced in the Old World before American settlement. After visiting the German, Scotch-Irish, and English farms, the museum walk concludes at the nineteenth century Valley farmsite, representing an American composite of these ethnic traditions. With the farms setting the stage for their interpretations of everyday rural life, the museum presents a living study of immigration and acculturation in the Valley. From an architectural vantage, it becomes clear, even to the untrained eye, that each ethnic group brought its own repertoire of building practices to the New World.

The influx of immigrants traveling along the Great Road from Pennsylvania into the Valley typified that most American stereotype: "the cultural melting-pot." Yet, the mixing of cultures in the New World occurred much earlier than many realize, beginning as early as 1680 along the Delaware River. In addition to the dominant groups of Germans, Scotch-Irish, and English, were the Swedes, Finns, Dutch, Welsh, and Native Americans. This is *not* to say that each cultural group actively embraced the others; to the contrary, they wished to remain separate. In the Valley, it was the confining geography and the sheer numbers of settlers that forced acculturation.

One factor common to many Germans and Scotch-Irish settling in the New World was their identity as religious dissenters. They did not belong to the Church of England and had been persecuted in their homelands. The Valley held the promise of free expression, even celebration, of their religious beliefs and ethnic heritage. This prompted an optimism which served to reinforce the practice of old traditions.

The traditional builder, whether German, Scotch-Irish, or English, held a *mental* representation of what a house should be and entertained a limited number of ways in which this mental model could be modified. Such modifications were typically governed by the builder's experience, the building materials available, and the special needs of the person for whom the house was to be built. For example, the abundance of trees in the New World heavily influenced Scotch-Irish builders to construct log and frame houses even though timber had been scarce in Northern Ireland. Yet despite these influences, the houses built by early carpenters and masons looked surprisingly like the ones they left at home.

All cultural expressions, including those found in architecture, were warmly welcomed within each ethnic community; they provided a much-needed source of comfort for a people struggling to adapt to the challenges of frontier life. This psychological interpretation of the factors governing traditional building practices suggests further that the obvious manifestations of cultural logic in early buildings were deliberately placed. Indeed, the desire to transform the unforgiving frontier into towns filled with houses that looked like the ones back home was a pervasive one, shaped not only by the wish to embrace one's own cultural heritage, but also shaped by the insecurities of starting over in a new world.

Unfortunately, the majority of early domestic buildings were hastily constructed, built of poor materials, and consequently, did not survive long. Much of what is known today about these early buildings stems from those few structures whose construction was enduring; their study has resulted in the identification of several culturally-typed house forms which dominated eighteenth century building practices in the Valley. To date, the most comprehensive analysis of these house forms has come from the exhaustive fieldwork of Ann McCleary working under the aegis of the VHLC. Yet, we must realize that the process of identifying specific house types is an inexact science.

Except for the earliest structures, it is a myth that most settlers took it upon themselves to build their own houses. Skilled craftsmen were actively recruited by communities and wealthy landowners to build houses and places of worship. Unlike contemporary builders, detailed plans and blueprints were not drawn-up; instead, houses were built from memory and a reliance upon familiarity of form, learned principles of joinery and design, and the builder's own day-to-day experience of how domestic space was organized.

The Germanic house form (variably described as the continental, Rhenish or *Flurkuchenhaus* design) was exemplified by a three-room floorplan clustered about a prominent central chimney. This plan was a purely functional one reflecting Germanic ways of living and organizing space. The front entry opened into a long, narrow room which served as the kitchen (or *kuche*); this was the largest room in the house. The area opposite the fireplace was partitioned off to produce a relatively square parlor in the front (known as the *stube*) and a smaller room to the rear (the *kammer*).

The center for nearly all domestic activity was the *kuche*; it was here in front of the large hearth that family members gathered to prepare meals, dine together, complete daily chores, and enjoy social activities. The *stube* might also have provided a place for doing chores and socializing in fair weather, whereas the *kammer* was typically reserved for storage. Sleeping arrangements depended upon the season; in the winter, the warmer corners of the house were reserved for the adults with the children typically sleeping in an upstair loft.

Viewed from the outside, this three-room floorplan was both familiar and easily recognizable to the German pioneer. The fenestration (i.e., placement of windows and doors) was

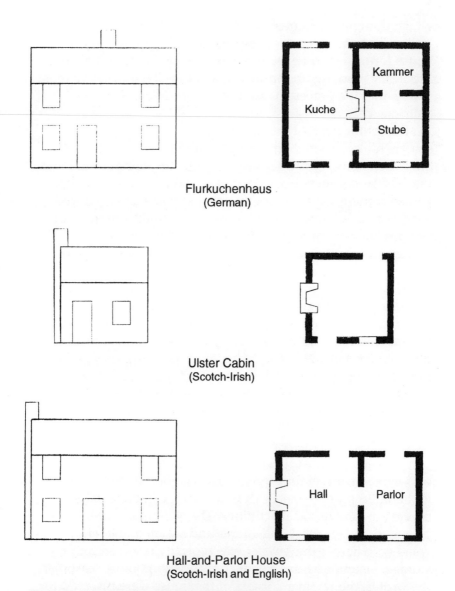

Flurkuchenhaus
(German)

Ulster Cabin
(Scotch-Irish)

Hall-and-Parlor House
(Scotch-Irish and English)

Figure 3. Examples of traditional floorplans found in the Valley of Virginia. The houses built by the first and second generations of German, Scotch-Irish, and English settlers in the Valley were similar in plan to those found in Europe just prior to the settlers' emigration to the New World. Note that unequal room sizes and an asymmetrical arrangement of windows in the facade were characteristic of these ethnically-typed house designs.

30

asymmetrically organized with the front door placed to one side and the chimney placed off-center according to the unequal sizing of the *kuche* and *stube*. Windows were a luxury item and were typically few in number; they, too, were organized asymmetrically according to room placement and size. Stone was the preferred building material for those who could afford it, although finely hewed log houses with full-dovetailed corner joinery were also popular. Finally, the outside dimensions were nearly square. Together, these physical characteristics gave the Germanic house a distinctive look. It was not a balanced facade, but rather a functional one. There were, of course, many variations on this general theme, including the addition of more rooms.

Although not located in Greenville proper, the large stone building located one mile to the north of town at the intersection of US Routes 11 and 340 has a three-room, Germanic floorplan and is similar in dimensions to the German-built houses found near Adam Miller's "Massanutting" in Rockingham County. Although it does not possess a central hearth, the gable-end chimneys were built within the side walls similar to acculturated Germanic designs found throughout Pennsylvania and the lower Valley. Admittedly, this stone structure is on a grander scale than the typical dwelling built by the German settlers. Known as the "Hessian House," its date of construction lies between 1790 and 1820.

The first identified owner of this property after the Beverley Grant was divided into parcels was Thomas Shields who sold seventy acres on Christians Creek (adjoining the property at the base of the hill to the east) to John Shields of Botetourt County. *Mutual Assurance Records,* dating 1803, describe a "stone dwelling" measuring 40 by 50 feet valued at $2500 plus a stone and wood mill also measuring 40 by 50 feet valued at $3500.

In noting that the current structure only measures 30 by 40 feet, several historians have concluded that the house was rebuilt or modified in the 1820s by George Crobarger who was deeded the land in 1810 by Agnes Shields. Yet the current dimensions of the Hessian House are similar to another

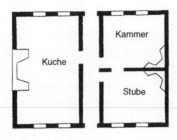

Kuche

Kammer

Stube

Figure 4. Hessian House, circa 1780–1820. Relatively square dimensions, stone construction with gable end chimneys built into the walls characterize this dwelling house. This is the front view of the house which was originally facing the road; US Route 340 was rerouted earlier this century so that only the rear of the house can now be seen from the road. The balanced placement of windows with a central doorway suggest that this is an acculturated Germanic design with an nineteenth century building date; however, the floorplan is a traditional, three-room with center hall, continental design reminiscent of Old World traditions.

Figure 5. Thomas Williams House, circa 1804. A center chimney, relatively square dimensions and a well-balanced facade identify this house as an acculturated Germanic design. The structure represents the only center chimney, two-room floorplan remaining in Greenville.

Augusta County stone dwelling named "Grey Gables," believed to have been built between 1779 and 1780 by Hessian mercenaries captured in the Revolutionary War. Apparently, they traveled to the Valley and marketed their stone masonry skills to prominent Augusta County farmers. It has been suggested that the Hessian House near Greenville was the product of these craftsmen; however, no evidence exists to support this theory. Hessian or not, the house is significant as it represents one of a few identifiable Germanic forms located in the Greenville area.

The only Germanic plan currently existent in Greenville proper is the Thomas Williams House located on the corner of US Route 11 and Virginia Route 1203. This modest log and frame house is rectangular, measuring 20 by 28 feet with a central chimney and symmetrical fenestration. The front door opens to a small passageway which leads to either the *kuche*

33

or *stube.*

The earliest reference to this house is found in a deed dated June, 1804, when the heirs of Thomas Steele conveyed the property to Thomas Williams wherein it is described as the "same lott James Williams now lives." Apparently, the Williams family had improved the land some time earlier; however, no earlier deeds exist. In contrast to the Hessian House, this dwelling is more representative of the buildings of the early settlers.

In contrast to the *Flurkuchenhaus,* Scotch-Irish building forms are not as clearly identifiable due to earlier adoption of English building traditions in the British Isles. Nevertheless, associations between the square log houses found throughout the upper Valley and the stone and mud dwellings found in Ulster have long been recognized. This Scotch-Irish form included a chimney located to one end with asymmetrical fenestration favoring a door placed to one side and a window, if present, dividing the remaining space.

Since many of the Scotch-Irish had been poor tenant farmers in Ireland, they possessed few building skills as a group. Their native houses in the Old World were typically of crude construction. Small stones, thatch and mud were typical building materials. A survey of tenant farmers living around Ulster in 1619 revealed "houses covered in clods," "a chimney at the end made with waddles," and "a fair cagework house" among others. There were exceptions, of course, as the gentry often built substantial stone buildings.

The Scotch-Irish settlers adopted the tradition of log construction from Scandinavian and German cultures upon arrival in the New World. However, the Ulster settlers avoided the more complicated center chimney designs of the Germans, opting instead to build a chimney externally on the gable end. In addition, the corner joinery of the early Scotch-Irish was crude, employing a single V-notch versus the precise full-dovetailing tradition of the Germans.

Several log houses resembling the Scotch-Irish design were built in Greenville. This should come as no surprise, as the area between Staunton and Timber Ridge was heavily settled by Ulster immigrants. Perhaps the earliest examples standing today are the buildings composing the William Smith Tavern property, dating back to 1782 or earlier. This property is located along the north bank of the South River on the east side of Greenville's Main Street.

The earliest log structure measures twenty feet square and contains a single room on the main floor, with an open staircase located opposite the fireplace, leading to a one-room loft. A second staircase led to the basement but has been removed. The former stair might have been enclosed at one time, as several tongue-and-groove wall boards remain — a common partition in Valley houses. Interior surfaces on all three floors show traces of lime white-wash suggesting that the logs and ceiling joists remained uncovered. Both the basement and first floor rooms originally contained a hearth, each measuring five feet across; the chimney was originally built of limestone.

The dwelling was built into a hill on a foundation of dry-laid stone, providing a full walk-in basement; the floor was bricked sometime in the mid-nineteenth century. This use of terrain to provide a cellar is an ancient practice, common to the Old World building traditions of the Germans and Swiss. The outside walls were constructed of hewed oak timbers with V-notch joinery at the corners. This construction allowed between two and six inches between the logs which were filled with wood chips and a sandy mortar mix. The current fenestration appears to be original and typical of the Ulster cabin with the front door located off-center and a single window dividing the remaining facade; however, the initial structure was probably built without windows. Although long gone, the original roof was made of oak shingles or "shakes."

Overall, the Smith Cabin contained three floors with one room on each. As in the Germanic *kuche,* the second or main floor provided the primary living space where food preparation, dining, and sleeping took place. The loft, easily accessible from the main room, was probably used for storage and extra sleeping space. The basement, too, provided cooking and storage space and was cool enough in the summer to

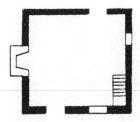

Figure 6. First Smith Tavern (cabin), circa 1742–1782. William Smith built this 20-foot-square log house; its single room floorplan and gable chimney at one end is a hallmark of the tenant dwellings found in Ulster. The use of the hillside to produce a stone, walk-in cellar reflects Old World Swiss and German traditions. The front door placement to one side is typical. The smaller windows are likely to be original (if there were any at all); the front double-hung window is an early nineteenth century addition. Note that a single V-notch characterizes the corner joinery; this is the most common method of log building in the upper Valley. This is the tavern building that the Marquis De Chastellux stopped at in 1782; the Ridge Road ran directly in front of the tavern in the early days.

keep perishables.

As might be expected for a "first" dwelling, the Smith Cabin was crudely built. It provides a good example of Scotch-Irish building while also revealing the rugged living conditions that the early settlers endured during the middle of the eighteenth century. That the cabin has not been razed is unusual. In contrast to the Hessian House, the survival of the Smith Cabin is not likely to be attributable to its sound construction but rather to having been valued, and therefore preserved, by the Smith family for nearly two-hundred years. In this regard, the cabin was improved several times during the nineteenth century. The large, inefficient hearth was replaced with a smaller flue suitable for a woodstove and an ell was added to the rear. The cabin was once sheathed with clapboards and a double-hung window was added to the facade. The clapboards have been removed and the ell was torn down many years ago leaving the Smith Cabin looking much as it did when first constructed.

A third building style common to both the Scotch-Irish and the English was the hall-and-parlor design. Subtle differences between the hall-and-parlor houses found throughout the Valley and those found in the Tidewater area suggest that the former was an acculturated design and not simply a transplanted house form carried to the Valley by the English settlers who crossed the Blue Ridge. In contrast to Tidewater hall-and-parlor designs, the Valley houses favored enclosed versus open staircases, single board versus post/beam wall partitions, and hewed-log versus brick construction. Wide use of brick for building Valley houses did not occur until the 1820s.

Like the Germanic and Ulster designs, the hall-and-parlor house had a front doorway opening into a large room called the hall, containing a fireplace designed for cooking on one side and a stairway in the opposite corner. The second room or parlor was smaller and often, but not always, had a fireplace of its own. Early hall-and-parlor houses often evidenced an asymmetrical fenestration with the doorway located off-center leading into the hall, but later forms showed a more balanced facade which concealed unequal room sizes inside. One or two windows were located on either side to divide the remaining space, often providing a three-bay facade. As before, functional considerations prevailed over stylistic ones in the earliest structures.

The second Smith Tavern building constructed between 1794 and 1801 is a hall-and-parlor design. This log structure was rectangular and measured 22 by 27 feet with a large limestone chimney situated on the north gable end. The facade was nearly symmetrical with three bays and a centered front door opening into the hall. This room was nearly sixteen feet square and was about twice the size of the parlor. The house was sheathed in decorative, beaded clapboards at an early date; oak shakes completed the roof.

The Tavern was modified by a log lateral addition in the early 1800s and two brick ells to the rear around 1830. All additions had fireplaces. The fenestration was changed to assimilate the lateral addition into a balanced five-bay facade. The front door was moved and now opens to an unheated center hall whereas before it led to the large north room served by the fireplace.

In its original configuration, the hall served as the primary living space; the parlor was a storage and sleeping room. Flexibility in room usage was increased if the parlor had its own fireplace, allowing this room to be used also for completing daily chores and sleeping in colder weather. Whereas the Germanic and Ulster floorplans became significantly less common in the nineteenth century, the hall-and-parlor design persisted well into the early twentieth century.

In addition to the hall-and-parlor house, there was an emerging English form gaining popularity among the well-to-do. This form was none other than the Georgian house plan, a Renaissance-inspired design composed of a large, two-room deep, rectangular block with a symmetrically organized facade. The floorplan included a center hall flanked by two rooms on each side. The Georgian form was not unknown to continental Europe, as it was derived from the "classical" architecture of the Roman empire; however, in the context of

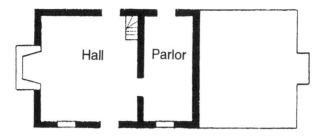

Figure 7. Second Smith Tavern, circa 1794–1801. The left three-fifths (from the doorway to the chimney) of this large building comprises the original log building. The doorway was initially located near the second window but was moved when the house was enlarged. Note that the upper and lower windows on the left side do not align, which is unusual. The large chimney is made from limestone and was used for hearth cooking. In its original configuration, the Tavern contained a large heated hall and a smaller parlor. This floorplan, with its unequal room sizes, was typical of early hall-and-parlor houses and is similar to houses found in England during the seventeenth and eighteenth centuries. The lateral addition (the remaining two-thirds to the right of the doorway) dates to around 1814 when the Smith family first acquired the building. The whole building was clapboarded soon after it was bought. The brick facade, an afterthought, was added in 1953.

influencing early American builders, the Georgian style, as the name implies, is considered to be of English origin.

The facade of the Georgian house was unmistakable. Windows and doors were arranged in perfect order. Such houses were immediately recognized as a symbol of wealth and stature. It was not uncommon to "disguise" older, less progressive houses behind a Georgian facade; for example, the second Smith Tavern building just discussed originally had a three-bay Georgian facade to impress the passerbys while a hall-and-parlor arrangement served its occupants on the inside.

The Georgian house was introduced by the gentry along the eastern seaboard in the early eighteenth century; some Virginia plantation houses built in the Tidewater area exhibited this style as early as 1725. The form appeared west of the Blue Ridge much later, and then was built only for the very rich. To accommodate the desire of less wealthy persons to own a contemporary house, the full Georgian model was often reduced in size by eliminating the rooms on one side of the central hall. This gave rise to the two-thirds Georgian house, or side-passage plan, which became very popular throughout Pennsylvania.

In Greenville, the southern part of the Henry Apple House represents a two-thirds Georgian plan; it is the only surviving example of this style with log construction in Augusta County. The house bears the name of Henry Apple who lived there in the 1930s. The VHLC estimated a building date of around 1820 with a lateral log addition to the north built some twenty years later. Deed and tax records suggest that a smaller house was built on the land in 1809 by John B. Mitchell. It is unclear whether or not this earlier structure was incorporated into the larger house.

In contrast to the designs discussed previously, the fenestration of the Apple House was organized to project a balanced facade with less emphasis placed upon functional attributes. Since the house consisted of only two-thirds of the complete Georgian ideal — that is a central hall and two rooms to one side only — the facade was unbalanced. Yet, the

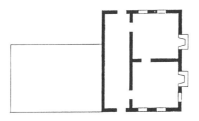

Figure 8. Henry Apple House, circa 1809–1820. The right half of the building comprises the original log structure. The fenestration is unaltered although the first floor windows have been enlarged. The rooms are unlabeled, as it is unclear how they were used. The front room probably served as the parlor, but the rear room could have been either a hall, bedchamber, or second parlor. It is likely that a separate building was used for preparing meals. As illustrated below, the "perfect" Georgian house facade had five bays (that is, the number of windows across the top) with a central doorway; it was a geometrically balanced design, both inside, with its central passageway, and outside, with its symmetrical fenestration. The complete design was broken down into fractional parts when a smaller Georgian house was desired, resulting in the side-passage or two-thirds Georgian model. The three-bay design (lower right) was a scaled-down version of the Georgian model; it was popular in the Valley, as it was affordable. The three-bay design mimicked the balance of the larger version with the advantage of being a complete idea and not a fractional type.

41

Georgian design was so high-style that even an incomplete facade was impressive.

It is unknown when the structure was covered with clapboards. Given its high-style design, it is possible that they were part of the original facade once the house was enlarged to produce the Georgian design. The beaded edging on the clapboards suggests an attention to detail common among better houses built in the early nineteenth century. The two large brick chimneys located on the south wall provided heat for all four of the original rooms — this was certainly a luxury compared to the cold loft of the Smith Cabin. The masonry construction of the chimneys is significant, as it dates the house in the late 1820s — about the time when brick construction first appeared in Greenville.

The Apple House was certainly an impressive structure along Greenville's Main Street in the early 1800s. In contrast to earlier house plans, the center for domestic activities in Georgian houses was located outside the formalized room arrangement, either in a detached kitchen or in the basement.

6

A River Settlement

The Greenville area adjoining the South River was settled soon after John Lewis established his homeplace at Bellefonte. When the Beverley land grant was divided into parcels and sold, the Greenville area was part of 1546 acres sold to Patrick Campbell on February 21, 1738. Patrick Campbell, born in 1696, was forty-two years old when he acquired the land. He had immigrated to the New World with his father, John Campbell (1674–?), and several adult brothers and sisters from Ireland in 1726, first settling in Lancaster, Pennsylvania, in 1733, and then moving to Augusta County (then Orange County) in 1738.

The 1546 acres originally conveyed to Patrick Campbell in 1738 were divided and the land that was to become Greenville changed hands four times before being purchased by Thomas Steele, one of the town's founders, in 1793. These conveyances are briefly detailed as follows:

> Patrick Campbell to William Sayers in 1745.
> William Sayers to John Patterson on October 24, 1748.
> John Patterson to John Ward on May 18, 1750.
> John Ward to John Sterling on March 20, 1775.

Thomas Steele purchased two-hundred-thirty acres located primarily along the south bank of the South River for six-hundred pounds "current money of Virginia" from John Sterling and his wife, Catharine, on November 28, 1793. This sale price works out to about 2.6 pounds per acre. To put this value into perspective, consider that as early as 1645 the

43

House of Burgesses established that a "Spanish piece of eight" (or one silver dollar) was equal to six shillings, and that twenty shillings was equal to one pound. Hence, each acre cost a little more than eight and one-half dollars.

This conveyance included an unspecified number of "premises" and was described according to its natural features as follows:

Beginning at two small white oaks on the south side of the south branch of Shenandoah river thence south one degree east one hundred and thirty poles to two tall hickorys, thence south fifty-six degrees west two hundred and sixty poles to the line of the aforesaid one thousand five hundred and forty six acres, thence with said lines north twelve degrees east three hundred and forty three poles to a stake, thence south sixty one degrees east eighty six poles to a white oak, thence south seventy six degrees east seventy two poles to a white oak, thence south thirty four and a half degrees west twenty poles to the beginning.

Despite the frequent changes in ownership between 1738 and 1793, the word "premises" suggests that the land along the South River was already the site of rudimentary development by the mid-1700s. This is not surprising given the favorable geographic features of the area.

The site which later became Greenville was characterized by a smooth, sloped bank leading to the southern edge of the river. This slope extended eastward with higher ground located to the west, providing excellent building sites overlooking the river. In contrast, the north bank was marked abruptly by twenty-foot bluffs, tapering to a gentler slope to the east, allowing access to a broad, flat plain along the river's edge. This descent along the bluffs, leading to the river's edge, offered a natural ford for crossing the river. This feature was of some importance given the dangers involved in trying to coax horses and livestock, not to mention pulling a loaded wagon, across swift moving rivers. The South River itself flowed eastward with a healthy vitality, meandering its way north. With the higher ground along its western banks, the river provided an ideal mill site just west of the ford. In addition, a lively spring (now called Gulliam Spring) emptied into the river along its south bank just seventy-five yards west

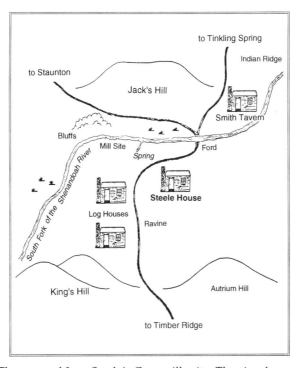

Figure 9. Thomas and Jane Steele's Greenville site. The site chosen in November 1793 to develop Greenville Town was characterized by a gentle hillside rising along the south bank of the river ford with a small ravine along its western edge; the whole area was surrounded by four prominent hills. Two roads circled around Jack's Hill from the north and met at the ford. The Ridge Road was part of the old Indian Road that passed Tinkling Spring, whereas the Staunton Road was an alternate route that became more popular as travel from Staunton increased. On the southside of the ford, the exact path of the Great Road is unknown. Here it is shown crossing the river just below the first Smith Tavern where it veered west along the river bank, thence following the ravine (along and slightly behind where Back Street or US Route 11 is located) and curving around King's Hill towards Staley's Hill. Greenville's present Main Street did not exist, as it was more practical to follow the ravine. Note that the Stuart-Hutchens House (labeled as the Steele House) faces the river, perhaps suggesting that the road ran to its front; other early cabins were probably located along the edges of the ravine in order to take of advantage of the hillside and to face the road. The plan of the town was influenced by a desire to straighten out the road from the ford, also allowing more lots to be surveyed. The hillside now occupied by the Main Street became more desirable once the road was rerouted as this land provided better water drainage and was less susceptible to river flooding.

45

of US Route 11. Greenville was surrounded by four hills whose names reflect previous events or landowners. The hill running east-west along the north border of town and punctuated by the aforementioned bluffs was known as "Jack's Hill." This hill was divided over time, as the path of the Valley Pike/US Route 11 was leveled and widened. The Great Road circled from the west, approaching the basin alongside the bluffs and followed their descent towards the river. This road is named the Old Staunton Road today and is the extension of the Old Greenville Road. A second early road ran along the ridge to the east and curved around the opposite end of Jack's Hill; the two roads met at the ford. This latter road is known as Indian Ridge Road. The gradual hill to the southeast of town and behind the current Greenville Methodist Church was named "Autrium Hill" whereas "King's Hill" is located to the immediate southwest and is the highest of Greenville's hills. Finally, to the southeast about one-half mile, the ridge running east-west is known as "Staley's Hill." As such, Greenville was flanked by hills.

Waddell described the naming of Staley's Hill in about the year 1800 as follows:

Several children going to school one morning, saw a traveler on horseback moving northward, who was overtaken by a man walking and carrying a gun. The two proceeded together for a while, and then the footman fell behind and deliberately shot and killed the other. Taking the traveler's saddlebags and mounting his horse, the murderer fled, and was never heard of afterwards. The victim proved to be a merchant from East Tennessee, named Staley, who was going to Baltimore to purchase goods.

The primary vocations in Augusta County during the 1760s were farming and animal husbandry. Hemp and wheat were the primary cash crops with over 100,000 pounds produced throughout Augusta County each year after 1770. Much of this crop was transported across the Blue Ridge via Jarman's Gap to Charlottesville and on to Fredericksburg and Alexandria. By the 1780s, the raising of horses, cattle and hogs rivaled agricultural concerns in Augusta County. Much of the land surrounding Greenville was cleared for planting and grazing; it has been estimated that twenty percent of farmlands were cleared in the upper Valley by 1790.

The region was more than just an isolated farming community however. As early as 1749, a "classical school" was located just north of the Old Providence churchyard about five miles southwest of Greenville. Some historians have suggested that this school was established as late as 1773 which represents the date that the school was moved to Timber Ridge. Founded by Robert Alexander, a college educated gentleman who moved to Augusta County in 1743, this grammar school flourished as many wealthy landowner/ farmers sent their children for an education similar to that available in the eastern cities. The term "classical school" implied that the instruction provided went beyond rudimentary reading, writing, and arithmetic; both Latin and mathematics were taught there. The school flourished, as the Scotch-Irish placed high value on education, particularly with regard to furthering the religious studies of its younger generations.

Several prominent members of the Greenville community, including Samuel Doak and John Breckenridge, attended this school. Initially named "Augusta Academy," the school was renamed "Liberty Hall" during the Revolutionary War and was later moved to Lexington in 1785. This school later became Washington College in 1813 and continues today as Washington and Lee University.

In addition to the classical school, the number of area residents grew large enough to support its own Presbyterian Church. In 1779, Bethel Church was founded on a small back road approximately five miles northwest of Greenville. Previously, the settlers along the South River had to travel nearly ten miles to the North Mountain Meeting House near Middlebrook. Many of them walked this distance every Sabbath. This journey constituted a considerable hardship for many members, yet repeated discussions about the problem within the congregation did not produce any solutions. The resulting frustration prompted several men, led by Colonel Robert Doak, to take the matter into their own hands. The following description of the minister's (Archibald Scott) discovery of Colonel Doak's actions is offered by Waddell:

As he was riding through the neighborhood he came unexpectedly upon a company of men putting up a large log building. Upon inquiry, he found it was designed as a meeting-house. The people worshipping at the old North Mountain Meeting House, had been talking about a new church building and a new position, but nothing had been decided upon by the congregation. Fearing lest evil might spring from this sudden movement of one part of the congregation, the young pastor says: "Are you not too fast, my boys?" "No" said Colonel Doak, "we will end the dispute by putting up the church." The church building was completed, and called Bethel, and the dispute was heard of no more.

This episode reveals Colonel Doak's forthrightness, and also underscores the readiness of the local residents to establish their own community.

Some comments about the Doak family are relevant here. David Doak was among the first Scotch-Irish settlers to the area having obtained 100 acres just west of present-day Greenville from William Beverley. His sons were Samuel and Robert.

Samuel Doak was educated at Princeton, commanded a Valley cavalry unit during the Revolutionary War, and later moved to the North Carolina and Tennessee frontier. Robert Doak remained in Augusta County all his life and distinguished himself several times over through his political zeal, military service, and religious devotion. He served as Justice of the Peace, High Sheriff of the County, and Virginia General Assembly Delegate. During the Revolutionary War, he rose to the rank of Colonel and commanded the ninety-third regiment of militia — a post he held until March, 1813. Waddell provided an insight into his character stating that Colonel Doak "was unconscious of approaching age and infirmity, and, panting for renown on new fields, felt offended" by his forced retirement. When he passed away in 1832, Colonel Doak left a considerable estate and was survived by several younger generations who would also distinguish themselves as leaders in the Greenville community.

As the Doaks and other families were establishing their farms in the surrounding areas, several log houses were built close to the South River and along the Great Road in Greenville. Among the earliest of these was the Smith Cabin already mentioned. It is unclear, however, when William Smith actually settled in the area.

The earliest estimate of Smith's arrival is supported by a deed dated 1742 that was donated to the Marshall Museum in Lexington, Virginia, by Mary Lyle Smith Crum — a descendant of William Smith who lived in the Tavern between 1952 and 1981. This deed indicates that Smith obtained a land grant directly from the English Crown and suggests that the eastern border of the Beverley patent was located along the outskirts of Greenville. Smith also purchased a 269 acre parcel from Samuel Braford on May 2, 1752, described as "lying or being on a headbranch of the South River." Originally, the tract had contained 538 acres that was conveyed to James Lynn in 1747 by William Beverley. In his will dated 1756, William Smith bequeathed his "plantation" to his two stepsons, Robert and Thomas Steele. This latter stepson is the same Thomas Steele who eventually purchased the land that was to become Greenville! Despite these difficulties in identifying exactly when William Smith settled near Greenville, it is clear that he, like Patrick Campbell and David Doak, was among the first settlers to establish a homeplace in the area.

The first dwelling was presumably the Ulster cabin built into the hillside, overlooking the north bank of the South River. A separate, two-story log house located at the river's edge was acquired by the Smith family in 1814. Historians have frequently made the mistake of assuming that William Smith built this second building and that it was existent before 1793. To the contrary, deed and tax records reveal that this house was built by either Abraham Troxel or Thomas Lyons sometime between 1794 and 1801. Although it is the larger log house that is heralded as the location of the tavern, the smaller log cabin on the hill housed tavern guests in earlier times.

Quite unlike the quaint bed-and-breakfast inns we find so appealing today, the early taverns or "ordinaries" were rarely more than an extra space in someone's loft. In large towns, tavern keepers were highly regarded and typically boasted of commodious accommodations. This was not true of rural tavern keepers. Although the costs for rooms and meals were fixed by the County court, there were no standards governing the quality of the accommodations to be provided. Waddel reported the tavern rates set in 1800 as follows:

Breakfast or supper, 25 cents; dinner, 42 cents; lodging per night, 12½ cents; servants diet, 16 cents; Maderia wine per quart, $1.25; port wine, 83 cents; sherry, $1; whiskey per gill, 4 cents; corn or oats per gallon, 12½ cents.

It was not uncommon for tavern visitors to endure sleeping alongside strangers upon lice-infested straw beds located in cold and drafty lofts. Moreau de Saint-Mary, a Frenchman traveling in America during the 1780s, once described white sheets as "the rarest of all things in every American tavern . . . for they [travelers] are expected to sleep between sheets on which the traces of previous occupants are encountered." Or as one eighteenth century tavern patron wailed, "It is a pity that the rats of the town hold court in this house." Meals, if available, consisted of whatever was on hand and were served in common dishes with few utensils.

William Smith's hillside cabin was well-situated along the Great Road at the South River ford to provide lodging for the many travelers headed to the frontier in the late 1700s. Licenses for at least one-hundred separate taverns had been granted by the Augusta County Court prior to the Revolutionary War. By 1800, there were several competing taverns located along the road between Staunton and Lexington.

Historians have long equated the Smith Tavern with the large two-story log house located near the river's edge. This building served as the site of the Smith Tavern and stagecoach stop after 1814 and throughout most of the nineteenth century until Civil War times. Brake related the following description of this Tavern collected from Mary Lyle Smith Crum, the last of a long line of Smiths who lived there until Mary's death in 1981.

She described the Tavern as a small room used to store whiskey and a larger adjacent room which served as the town Post Office. Another room next to the post office room was used as a bedroom since this was a stage coach stop and necessary to provide shelter at times for a passenger stopping over. An interesting feature of this tavern was a small window on the North side immediately adjacent to the bar used to hand out mail and bottles of whiskey as people were mainly on horseback. A counter below the window had a slot cut through into a drawer. The money paid for whiskey was put into the drawer through this slot and the drawer was kept locked.

This description of the rooms underscores the social importance of the tavern. Catering primarily to males, taverns were loud and smoky places stocked with hard liquor. Cock fights, tests of physical strength, and gambling were popular; fist fights were frequent among its well-sauced patrons. Taverns also provided a vital link to the outside world, as visitors brought news from Staunton and beyond.

Sometimes the thirst for news on the part of the locals was overwhelming to travelers as described in 1780 by Englishman, George Grieve:

At an inn, the scrutiny is minute; your name, quality, the place of your departure, and object of your journey, must all be declared to the good family in some way or other, for their credulity is equal to their curiosity, before you can sit down in comfort to the necessary refreshment. This curious spirit is intolerable in the eastern states.

Inside, the Smith Tavern was likely to have been a dimly-lit place with a strong human odor. Notices of all shapes and sizes sheathed its dark log walls. Many teamsters made it a regular stop to feed and rest their horses while they drank and socialized. Overnight business was typically heavy in the warmer months with many families making the journey west. So heavy was the traffic along the Great Road by the first quarter of the nineteenth century, that it probably contributed to the Smith Tavern being improved with several large brick and frame additions. Certainly, it remained the center of activity during Greenville's formative years.

Aside from the Tavern buildings, another pre-Revolutionary War structure located in Greenville is the Stuart Hutchens House which was surveyed by the WPA in the mid-1930s. The name is of the house's owner between 1914 to 1962.

According to an oral history collected during the survey, this structure was described as the oldest house "now standing in Greenville." The WPA report lists 1836 as an estimated building date which is inconsistent with their reported oral history suggesting that the date is in error. In fact, the deed and will records reveal that this property was never sold as an unimproved lot following the surveying of Greenville in 1793. It is possible that some portion of this house was contemporaneous with the Smith cabin. Unfortunately, since the dwelling was apparently inhabited by renters before 1793, no deeds exist to trace its origins.

Figure 10. Stuart Hutchens House, circa 1742–1794. Like the first Smith Tavern, this log house was built into the hillside. It is a rectangular structure with its gable end facing Greenville's Main Street — an unusual orientation suggesting that it faced an older roadway to its front (no record of the house having ever been moved exists). The floorplan consists of a hall and parlor. Its original chimney, once located along the west gable wall, has long since been removed and replaced by a smaller flue suitable for a woodstove. The original cooking hearth was located in the basement. This house was originally owned by the Steele family and was not sold during the first and second wave of lot purchases in 1794 and 1795. As such, it probably predates the establishment of Greenville.

The Stuart Hutchens House is an L-shaped structure of log construction with a frame addition to the rear. Its three brick chimneys are recent additions dating to the mid-to-late nineteenth century. Like the Smith Tavern, the house stands relatively close to the South River, on the south bank and west of Main Street. Oral histories collected by the WPA indicated that the Breckenridges, who were among the earliest settlers to Augusta County, lived there during the Revolutionary War.

This reference to the Breckenridge family bears mention, as this family, descendants of Alexander Breckenridge who settled in Augusta County in the 1730s, is well-known in local and national politics. Although no records exist to place the family in the house, it is noteworthy that Robert Breckenridge (grandson of Alexander) lived near Staunton in the 1760s, and his son, John, was educated at Liberty Hall in the 1770s. Perhaps he lived in Greenville during this period. The family did own considerable acreage in southern Augusta County. John Breckenridge later became Attorney General of the United States in Thomas Jefferson's administration (1800 to 1809).

When Greenville was founded, Thomas Steele maintained ownership of the Stuart Hutchens property, but the house was the residence of William Steele. Tax records indicate that the Stuart Hutchens House was one of the most valuable properties in 1801 at which time the log house was probably already improved with frame additions. Thomas Jackson became the new owner in 1814.

Another reputedly early building is the Samuel Finley House, located on the southside of Main Street on lots 4 and 5 and described by the WPA survey as having been constructed in the 1760s. According to Mutual Assurance Records of 1802, the house was a two-story "wood" building, measuring 54 feet long by 22 feet wide, with a center chimney. The center chimney design suggests that the house was elongated via a lateral addition on the side containing a gable-end chimney. The house was insured for $1700 and included a one-story detached (but with "cover way") kitchen, measuring 18 by 14

Figure 11. Samuel Finley House, circa 1797–1800. Only a portion of the original house survives, hidden behind new weatherboarding, a two-story porch, and a Victorian turret. The Mutual Assurance records of 1802 described the dwelling as a frame structure at a time when most other buildings in Greenville were built of logs; it was probably the first frame house built in Greenville. Consequently, it was highly valued by county tax assessors and was the only house in town with fire insurance. The diagram describes the property as it existed in 1802. This house served as a tavern in the early years and became Greenville's premier hotel after the Civil War. In 1909, the building was cut in half to make two separate houses; the northern part (the largest portion) burned early this century.

feet, with a value of one-hundred dollars. A second Assurance Bond, dated September 1805, revalued the house at $2100 and described the detached kitchen as having one and a half stories, measuring 14 by 10 feet. Such discrepancies in dimensions are hard to evaluate and may reflect either errors in measurement or actual changes in size. The 1805 document also showed a small "smoke house" to the south-rear of the house and a "lumber house" situated along the road next to the south wall of the house.

Since the deed records list no dwelling house or premises on this property prior to 1794, and tax records suggest a date as early as 1800, the WPA estimate is suspect. The house was probably built between 1797, the date when Finley purchased the property, and 1800. This property was judged by the county tax assessor to be the most valuable in Greenville from 1801 until the 1820s. In this regard, it is significant that the Finley House was the first frame house built in town and was probably the only frame house built before 1800. Finley operated a tavern as early as 1807 in this building — a use which continued until the late 1800s under a series of successive owners.

Among the other buildings thought to pre-date the development of Greenville in 1793 is the Thomas McKirgan House, a log dwelling rumored to have the date "1792" carved into one of its rafters. From the outside, the house appears to be unaltered except for a small, twentieth century addition to the rear. However, there is evidence (old mortise joints in the logs which are arranged in a random fashion) to suggest that the house was reconstructed on this site from another building. Consequently, the carved date might refer to this previous structure. Unfortunately, the current owners, Laurence and Karen Reed, have been unable to locate the carved date, and so it exists only as hearsay.

Thomas McKirgan purchased lots 4 and 5 on Back Street in 1804. In the deed for the former, it referred to the property as "being the same lot said McKirgan now lives." This notation suggests that McKirgan was living there prior to his purchasing the lot. The selling price for lot 4 was exorbitant and suggests that the dwelling was included in the sale price. The building was probably already reconstructed at this early date since the value is consistent with a "better" house.

The interior of the McKirgan House was quite contemporary for a log building with a single gable end chimney. Its Federal-style mantels, chair rails, and six-panel doors were hallmarks of affluent households in the early 1800s. The floorplan includes a center hall, which would have been quite progressive for 1804. The house was possibly reconfigured in the 1830s, but nevertheless a substantial log dwelling was present in 1804.

Figure 12. Thomas McKirgan House, circa 1792–1804. This is one of the oldest houses in Greenville. Random mortises in the logs suggest that this house was reconstructed from an earlier building built prior to 1804. The rumor of the date 1792 being carved on an attic rafter is unsubstantiated. Nevertheless, this building may have stood along the Great Road prior to the laying of lots in Greenville. The dimensions are similar to those of the Thomas Williams House leading some to speculate that the same builder is responsible for both houses; however, the Thomas McKirgan House is heated by a single gable end chimney; a cooking hearth was located in the cellar. It has a three-room, central passageway floorplan similar to the Hessian House.

Although only the Smith Cabin and the Stuart Hutchens House possess a documented history before 1793, it is likely that other early houses were built along the river and the Great Wagon Road which did not survive long enough to be documented. In fact, one of the chief conclusions of the VHLC survey of Augusta County historical resources was that few pre-1800 buildings have survived. Similar surveys in other areas, including Tidewater Virginia and New England, suggest that as few as ten percent of the original houses survive today. Both Peyton and Waddell have lamented about the poorly constructed, nearly uninhabitable dwellings first built by settlers in the Valley.

Despite strong development of the area between Greenville and Timber Ridge by the 1750s, all points south of Staunton were considered to be extremely primitive at the time. In fact, well into the 1790s, most of the developments in the upper Valley, including Staunton, were described as "crude," in a "pioneer state," and labeled as the "backwoods of Virginia." James Ireland, a Baptist minister, provided a general description of the people as "uncultivated," "rude and illiterate," and "a compound of the barbarian and Indian."

The roads were aptly described by a traveling Moravian Brethren in his diary entry dated October 24, 1753: " . . . immediately behind Augusti courthouse, the bad road begins" (referring to the Great Road south of Staunton). The hardships of wagon travel along this "bad" road were detailed in a second entry: "...the road ran up and down continually, and we had either to push the wagons or keep it back with ropes which we had fastened to the rear. There was no lack of water, for every two miles we met creeks." Even thirty years later, "Great Road" was considered to be a misnomer, as it continued to be described as overgrown, riddled with rocks and ravines, and impassable with mud when wet. In 1786, Count Castiglione described the going as so rough on the Great Road that his carriage "broke into a hundred pieces," discouraging him from traveling any further.

Unfortunately, specific accounts of the pioneer settlement

along the South River before 1793 are rare. There is one well-documented account describing the Greenville area in 1782. It comes from the diary of the Marquis De Chastellux, a Major General with the French troops sent to aid the patriots. He traveled extensively throughout the Middle Atlantic states following the Revolutionary War. In the spring of 1782, he crossed the Blue Ridge at Rockfish Gap and, as Waddell described, had much difficulty finding comfortable accommodations.

The Marquis and his party forded South River, where Waynesboro now is, and put up for the night at a little inn kept by a Mrs. Teaze, of which Mr. Jefferson had told him. He says the inn was one of the worst in all America. A solitary tin vessel was the only wash-bowl for the family, servants, and guests. The travelers did not pass through Staunton, but hurried on to a better inn than Mrs. Teaze's, promised them near the site of Greenville. They were doomed to disappointment, as the landlord, Mr. Smith, had neither food for the men nor forage for the horses. The war just closed had impoverished the country to that extent. Mr. Smith encouraged the party, however, to expect supplies at a mill further on.

The party went on to Steele's Tavern (also called Midway), but that is another story. The Smith Tavern referred to in this account was undoubtedly the small cabin on the hillside.

7

Revolutionary War

Throughout the Revolutionary War the Valley, and Greenville in particular, was too remote to experience enemy occupation. Yet, in June, 1781, the threat of invasion was acute. In
a well-documented drama, the Virginia General Assembly
fled, first from Richmond, and then from Charlottesville (at
Monticello), to the Augusta Parish Church in Staunton to
escape capture by Colonel Banastre Tarleton and his west-
ward-moving British Army. The General Assembly conducted its legislative business in Staunton from June 7th to
the 23rd before fleeing again when news arrived that Tarleton
was on the march, heading for Rockfish Gap. One account has
it that Patrick Henry hurried out of Staunton with such haste
that he left wearing only one boot.

Waddell provided the following account of the alarm
which spread through the upper Valley on Sunday, June 10,
1781.

*On Sunday, the people of Tinkling Spring congregation were as-
sembled as usual for worship, when a strange man, arrested in the vicinity,
was brought to the church. This man was one of four who had been
captured, but the others had escaped. He was dressed partly in the uniform
of a British soldier, and was supposed to be a spy sent forward by Tarleton.
The excitement at the church may be imagined. The pastor, Rev. James
Waddell, addressed the congregation, urging the men to obtain arms and
hasten to Rockfish Gap, intending to go with them. . . . The alarm having
arisen, riders traversed the county to notify people. From Lexington to the
Peeked Mountain, now Massanutten, the people were aroused. The men
hastened to Rockfish Gap, while the women and children hid their silver*

spoons and other portable articles of value.

The British invasion never materialized, but it certainly caused quite a stir throughout the upper Valley. These events prompted a most memorable quote, as Peyton related that when General George Washington heard of the rally of Augusta men to Rockfish Gap, he exclaimed, " . . . leave me but a banner to plant upon the mountains of Augusta, and I will rally around me the men who will raise our bleeding country from the dust and set her free!"

Despite having been bypassed by invading armies, Augusta sent many men to war. In 1775, the Virginia Convention organized the counties of Buckingham, Amherst, Albemarle, and Augusta into a single military district, requiring them to raise a battalion of five-hundred men, ages sixteen to fifty, with appointed officers. Such recruitments continued throughout the war.

Militia duty was not new to Augusta County men; since the French and Indian wars, all able-bodied free men over twenty-one were required to avail themselves to the call of locally appointed captains if necessary. According to Waddell, every militiaman was to "furnish himself with a good rifle, if to be had, otherwise with a tomahawk, common firelock, bayonet, pouch, or cartouch box, and three charges of powder and ball." Unfortunately, most Augusta County farmers did not have, and could not afford, these accoutrements. As such, men reported for duty bringing a wide variety of weapons including farm implements, tools, knives, and firearms — some in good repair and some rudely deteriorated.

Military drills had been held annually in Augusta County, much to the enjoyment of those who came to watch. Far from being a serious training exercise, the event was more akin to a carnival. After a morning of tripping over each other while marching in formation, the drill typically deteriorated into a party complete with impromptu sporting, gaming, and heavy drinking. It was a reprieve from the hard toiling on the farm.

Men from the Greenville area participated in many expeditions both on the western frontier against the Indians as well as on numerous battle fronts from North Carolina to New Jersey. As such, they received considerable drilling as the war dragged on. Fortunately, each enlistment lasted only a period of months, allowing many men to return home throughout the war. Repeat enlistments were common. Just about every available man in Augusta County served in the Continental Army at some time during the War.

Of particular interest are the patriots from the Greenville area. The Campbell family, who originally obtained the land around Greenville from William Beverley, achieved distinction through the actions of Patrick Campbell's grandson, General William Campbell, who led his troops to victory against the English at the battle of Kings Mountain in South Carolina. He married Patrick Henry's sister, Elizabeth, after the war, and was further honored by having a Virginia county named for him (Campbell County, founded in 1782).

Perhaps the most famous Valley patriot, as far as Greenville is concerned, was Captain James Tate who organized a company formed from the Bethel and Tinkling Spring congregations in late 1780. This company was known as the "Augusta Riflemen."

Captain Tate was the eldest of five sons who traveled with John Tate, Sr., and wife from Ireland, via Pennsylvania, to Augusta County around 1745. Soon after the family settled near Greenville, the brothers married into very prominent families including the Doaks and Finleys. James Tate married Sally Hall, the granddaughter of the esteemed Judge and Virginia Senator Archibald Stuart of Staunton. His brothers (William, Thomas, John, and Robert) served in the militia during the Revolutionary War and afterwards distinguished themselves in public service, attaining such offices as Justice of the Peace and Virginia General Assembly Delegate. Before the War, Captain Tate owned and operated a mill near Greenville. As Peyton venerated, the family "was noted for its piety, industry and public spirit, was associated with the early efforts of the founder to improve the country, and is allied by marriage with some of the principal families of the county."

In January, 1781, the Augusta Riflemen led by Captain James Tate mustered at Waynesboro and marched into the Carolinas, via Lynchburg, under the command of Brigadier General Daniel Morgan. In South Carolina, they joined General Nathanael Greene's Continental Army. The company fought victoriously in the Battle of Cowpens on January 17, 1781, as described by Waddell.

The victory at Cowpens was one of the most remarkable of the war. Only twelve of the Americans were killed and sixty wounded. Of the enemy, ten commissioned officers were killed, and more than a hundred rank and file; two hundred were wounded; twenty-nine officers and more than five hundred privates were taken prisoners, besides seventy wagons.

In short, Colonel Tarleton's British Army was thoroughly routed at Cowpens.

The three-month enlistment of the Augusta Riflemen expired soon after, so they marched back to Shenandoah County via Rockfish Gap with the prisoners in tow. The Company returned to Augusta County after less than a month's absence — all returned home as heroes.

Their discharge was short-lived. Due to intensified enemy activity following Cowpens, Captain Tate was ordered to lead the Riflemen back onto the field of battle. As before, many Greenville men, including Ensign Robert Doak, were members of this reformed company. The subsequent battle at Guilford Courthouse (now Greensboro) in North Carolina on March 15, 1781, was costly, as Tate and many of his men were killed. Yet, the British Army, under the generalship of Lord Cornwallis, lost so many men that they were compelled to retreat. This action was strategic, as Cornwallis was unable to move northward to join the British forces in New England. This failure to regroup contributed to his defeat at Yorktown in October later that year.

Captain Tate's reputation as a hero was only strengthened by his death at Guilford Courthouse, as he reportedly held his ground despite the British onslaught. His command was completely surrounded, when he "received a ball which broke his thigh." Tate's actions on the battlefield were the result of a curious happenstance, as it has been noted that he suffered from "a little deafness," and did not hear the order given for his militia to retreat. The ensuing loss was deeply felt at home; Waddell noted that there were eight or ten widows in the bounds of Bethel congregation following the battle.

In addition to providing militiamen, Augusta County provided foodstuffs to the Revolutionary armies. But the demand for food was so great that resources were rapidly depleted. Most items of military value were commandeered by roaming commissary officers. On occasion, the Augusta County court provided monies to support families of soldiers. Certainly the account of the Marquis De Chastellux provided earlier underscored the scarcity of provisions in Greenville immediately following the War.

Despite the hardships of war and the subsequent economic depression wrought on the region, the conflict had a profound psychological effect upon the evolving Valley community. There emerged a deepfelt sense of pride among those who had endured the War. This brought people together, and for the first time, prompted a strong spirit of unity throughout the upper Valley. What was once a frontier buffer zone made up of poor immigrants and dissenters was now a community with its own history and aspirations.

It is not surprising that residents looked among themselves to define their heroes. Most men maintained their military titles during civilian life, attaining for themselves a position of social esteem not unlike that found in traditional English society. Others could gain entrance into the gentry through association. Consequently, social distinction came within the reach of many who would otherwise never have met the rigid qualifications of heredity required by the English. The desire for social recognition was so acute that several historians have remarked that the retention of military titles became so commonplace following the War as to cause much alarm and consternation among English visitors to America.

This reaction was clear in the comments of Isaac Weld, an

English traveler to the upper Valley in 1796:

In every part of America a European is surprised at finding so many men with military titles, but nowhere, I believe, is there such a superfluity of these military personages as in the town of Staunton; there is hardly a decent person in it, excepting lawyers and medical men, but what is a colonel, a major, or a captain.

Weld would have found this state of affairs to be the same in Greenville.

It was during this postwar social climate that many new communities like Greenville, Middlebrook, and Brownsburg were established in the upper Valley. Placenames like Greenville and Waynesboro, both named for American Generals, further underscored the pride and unity felt by all who lived there. The trials of the frontier experience, coupled with the baptism of war, served to galvanize acculturation in the Valley. A new culture defined by place was emerging.

8
Founding of Greenville

The following account of the naming of Greenville has appeared with only minor variation in several sources, the earliest being a 1940 article in the *Staunton News Leader* by Nellie Drexel. The primary source is thought to be a 1922 school paper written by Samuel Alexander Doak McKee. As the story goes, some time around 1793, several residents gathered to incorporate the town, elect a mayor, and select a name. The majority opinion was to call the town Jacksonville after Captain Robert Jackson, a local Revolutionary War hero and prominent owner of land along the South River. Jackson declined the honor and suggested that the honor should go to General Nathanael Greene, under whom many of them had served during the battle of Cowpens in 1781. Following a majority vote, the settlement became known as Greenville.

It is likely that this town meeting occurred in anticipation of the surveying and offering for sale of lots beginning in December, 1793, only one month after Thomas Steele acquired the land for the town. Since many of the lots were unimproved, it is not clear who the residents were that attended the meeting. Perhaps only the trustees met in late 1793 to choose a name. Note that over the years, Greenville has been misspelled as Greensville; the latter spelling, however, does not represent an early form of the name.

The exact date when Greenville became officially recognized as a town is unclear. Greenville was the second town platted in Augusta County following Staunton, although many sources describe Waynesboro (platted in April, 1798, but previously known as Teases or Teasville) as having that distinction. Greenville was not incorporated and did not have a mayor until 1883.

No early surveys of Greenville exist despite references to a town plat in several early conveyances beginning in June, 1794. An advertisement dated December 20, 1793, in *The Staunton Spy* described the selling of lots in Greenville suggesting that the town was surveyed at that time. This advertisement read as follows:

We the undernamed subscribers being appointed trustees for the town of Greenville, laid-out in the county of Augusta, on the main road leading from Staunton to Lexington - have at present a considerable number of lots, containing one-fourth of an acre each - which they are determined to dispose of, on the most reasonable terms to such as will to become purchasers. The said town is laid out on a fine stream, and in a healthy, beautiful and opulent part of the country; so that, from its many particular advantages, there may be every expectation of its becoming a place of considerable commerce and traffic. Trustees: William Brownlee, James Mitchell, John Doak, Robert Doak, John Hawpe.

Six months following the appearance of this advertisement, the Augusta County court records show seven lots sold on June 17, 1794. The selling price was six pounds per lot. These lots were probably sold throughout the spring but were recorded on the same date as was common in those days since court recording of deeds was held infrequently. The first eight lots sold are listed as follows:

> John Mitchell - Lot 1 on the south-side of Main Street.
> Thomas Mitchell - Lot 2 on the south-side of Main Street.
> Robert Doak - Lot 3 on the south-side of Main Street.
> John Doak - Lot 3 on the north-side of Main Street.
> William McKee - Lot 4 on the north-side of Main Street.
> Abraham Troxel - Unnumbered lot on the south-side of Main Street, along the south bank of the South River.
> Adam Hawpe - Unnumbered lot on the north-side of Main Street, along the north bank of the South River.

It is important to note that the Troxel deed referred to above was recorded incorrectly; the parcel was located along the north bank of the South River. This error was corrected in later conveyances.

The prices paid for these lots represented a handsome profit for Thomas Steele given the previous purchase price of 2.6 pounds-per-acre he paid less than a year earlier. However, as emphasized in the 1793 newspaper advertisement, the land was very desirable. The area provided a natural fording spot to cross the South River, an ideal mill site, and a spring feeding into the river. These natural qualities were not lost on the trustees of the town. Clearly, speculative development of the area contributed to the creation of Greenville. In fact, commercial development of private land was encouraged by the Virginia General Assembly through a laissez-faire policy of recognizing new towns via individual petitions.

Nine additional lots sold during the next year were recorded on June 16, 1795. These conveyances included:

> Robert Steele - Lot 4 on the south-side of Main Street.
> Nathaniel Burkett - Lot 6 on the north-side of Main Street.
> Michael Apple - Lot 7 on the north-side of Main Street.
> John Moore - Lot 8 on the north-side of Main Street.
> Jacob Long - Lot 9 on the north-side of Main Street.
> Jacob Long - Lot 10 on the south-side of Main Street.
> George Shultz - Lot 11 on the south-side of Main Street.
> John Collins - Lot 12 on the south-side of Main Street.
> John Bright - Lot 14 on the south-side of Main Street.

By 1810, twenty-eight lots in Greenville had been sold. Back Street, running to the west and parallel to Main Street from the South River and joining Main at the south edge of town, was first mentioned in a series of deeds dated June 22, 1804. These conveyances included:

> Thomas Williams - Lot 3 on Back Street for $20.
> Thomas McKirgan - Lot 4 on Back Street for $400.
> Thomas McKirgan - Lot 5 on Back Street for $40.
> John Aston - Lot 6 on Back Street for $20.
> Jenny Tate - Lot 10 on Back Street for $20.
> Jacob Cline - lot 11 on Back Street for $20.
> John Smith - Lot 11 on the north-side of Main Street.
> John Smith - Lot 12 on the north-side of Main Street.

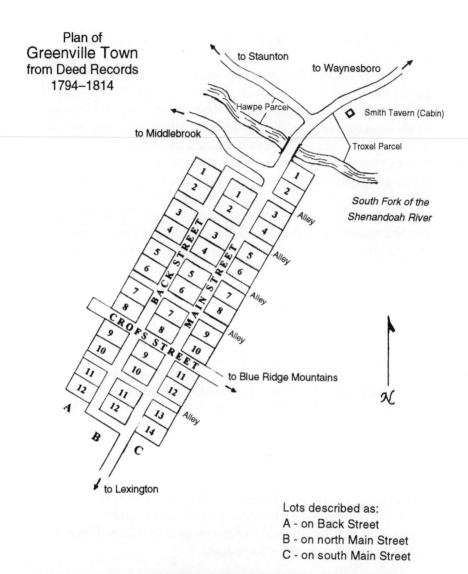

Plan of
Greenville Town
from Deed Records
1794–1814

to Staunton

to Waynesboro

Hawpe Parcel

to Middlebrook

Smith Tavern (Cabin)

Troxel Parcel

South Fork of the
Shenandoah River

BACK STREET

MAIN STREET

CROSS STREET

Alley

Alley

Alley

Alley

Alley

to Blue Ridge Mountains

Alley

N

A

B

C

to Lexington

Lots described as:
A - on Back Street
B - on north Main Street
C - on south Main Street

Figure 13. Plan of Greenville Town. Town lots in Greenville were organized in a gridiron pattern along its two principal streets — Main Street and Back Street. Each lot measured five by eight poles (excepting two lots located on the north bank of the river). All 38 lots were sold by 1814, just over twenty years after the first lots were offered for sale in December, 1793. The lots were numbered according to their street location and were described as being on: A) Back Street, B) North Main Street, or C) South Main Street.

68

The price for an unimproved lot was twenty dollars in 1804, with the six-pound price last appearing in 1799. The lots purchased by Thomas McKirgan included buildings. The well-appointed house mentioned earlier (circa 1792 ?) might represent the building on lot 5, as log houses, unless extravagant, were not of high value.

As seen in the early plat of the town reconstructed from the first decade of *Deed Book* records 1794 to 1804, Greenville was built along the Great Road which was designated as the Main Street. A smaller road running parallel to the west was called Back Street. Several ten-foot alleyways, running east-west, were placed between each pair of lots to connect Main with Back Street and to provide access to the side of each lot. Finally, a single street, aptly known as Crofs Street (an alternate spelling for cross) intersected both Main and Back streets in the southern half of town and led eastward to the base of the Blue Ridge Mountains.

This orthogonal or "gridiron" town plan was widely accepted in Virginia and was employed for nearly all turnpike towns in the Valley. In fact, gridiron plans were officially favored by the Virginia Colonial government as far back as the 1662 *Act for Building a Town*. Chief among the advantages of a gridiron was its ease of execution and expandability. Perhaps it reflected an ambitious optimism that the town might prosper and grow larger. These factors, plus the contours of the land and the importance of the road which ran through the middle, shaped its design. In this regard, the plan placed a uniform focus along the entire length of the Main Street — clearly a desirable attribute for a town developed along a major trade and travel route. This plan is similar to those of neighboring towns including Middlebrook and Mount Sidney.

No official record of any lots set aside for public use can be found. It is curious that the parcel bordering the north side of the road and lying along the south bank of the river was not sold. According to the town plan, this land would have consisted of the land between lot 1 on the north side of Main Street and the river. The road leading to Back Street and continuing west towards Middlebrook ran through here, but apparently the area between it and the river was open for public access to the water's edge.

Each numbered lot measured five by eight poles and contained one-quarter acre. (A pole equals 16½ feet.) Two lots adjoining the South River were larger than a quarter-acre and were initially unnumbered. These lots included the Abraham Troxel and Adam Hawpe parcels. Lots bearing the same number were described as being either south of Main Street, north of Main Street, or on Back Street.

The Smith Tavern property has not traditionally been considered to be part of Greenville proper, but has appeared intermittently on the town's tax list, presumably as a matter of convenience beginning in 1814; this was the year that the Smith family acquired the Troxel parcel. Note that the Troxel land was described in the original deed as "a certain lott in the town of Greenville." Hence, the larger log building was located in town whereas the Smith Cabin was not.

It is important to remember that several buildings, such as the Stuart Hutchens House, predated the laying of lots in Greenville. The first conveyance for this property following Thomas Steele's original purchase of Greenville lands in 1793 was recorded in 1799 in a will from Thomas to William Steele. The house was inhabited by the Steele family at the time of Greenville's development. In some cases, early buildings might have occupied parts of two town lots; perhaps this explains why the McKirgan House was rebuilt, using logs from a previous house or barn, on lot 5, Back Street. Conversely, it bears noting that lot sales did not reflect building activity, as town lots were often purchased for speculative reasons. Several of the trustees bought lots *in good faith* of the town's eventual success, although it is likely that few actually planned to live in town.

All original lots sold before 1799 were conveyed by Thomas and Jane Steele. After the death of Thomas Steele in 1799 (he was fifty-three years old), the lots were conveyed by his heirs. These heirs included Jane the widow, John and Jane Moore, William Steele, James and Rosanna Lyle, Hugh and

Sarah Young, Robert Steele, and Thomas and Catharine Jackson. Thomas and Catharine Jackson acquired most of the land surrounding and to the southeast of Greenville as indicated in a survey presented to the Chancery Court dated 1837. This settlement left seventeen acres and a town lot to Susan Peyton, fifty-three acres to Thomas T. Jackson, fifty-four acres and a town lot to William S. Jackson, seventy-seven acres and four town lots to Robert S. Jackson, and eighty-nine acres and a town lot to Mary L. Jackson. Together, this acreage surrounded all of Greenville and included seven town lots. Over time, Thomas Jackson's heirs sold off parcels of this land to Greenville residents, who more often than not purchased land adjoining the rear of their town lots. Catharine Jackson, Thomas' widow, remained in Greenville until her death in August of 1874, at age ninety, when she was reportedly the "oldest inhabitant" in town.

The role of the town's Trustees is unclear, as all the lots were conveyed directly from the Thomas Steele estate. It is likely that they supervised the surveying and selling of lots. Perhaps the trustees had encouraged Thomas Steele to purchase the land in the first place as a business venture to stimulate economic growth in the area. That the land was purchased only one month prior to the offering of town lots suggests there was a preconceived plan to develop the land. The trustees might have contributed monies to this end with Thomas Steele acting on their behalf.

All five of the original trustees were prominent land owners in the Greenville area. As such, all were in good financial shape to invest in the development of a new town. The tax records for 1800 reveals the following land holdings for each trustee: William Brownlee - 183 acres to the south of Greenville, John Doak and Robert Doak - 307 and 380 acres respectively to the southwest of Greenville, John Hawpe - 250 acres to the west of Greenville, and James Mitchell - 539 acres to the northwest of Greenville. In addition, will records reveal that these landowners continued to be prosperous; each left large holdings of livestock, personal property, and slaves when they passed on.

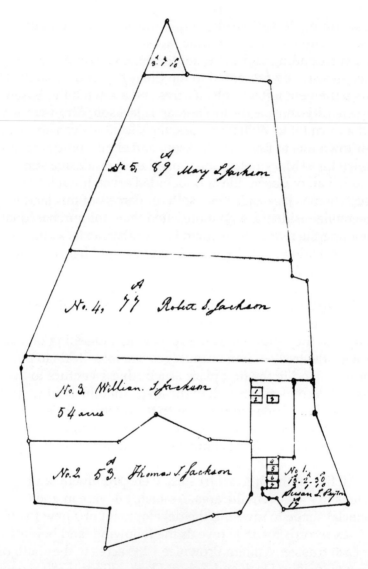

Figure 14. Lands of Thomas Jackson, 1837. Augusta County Chancery Court records detailing the settlement of the Thomas Jackson estate include this survey of the land surrounding Greenville. Clearly, Jackson was one of the chief landlords at the time, as he owned nearly all the land bordering the town, totaling 290 acres plus seven town lots. Just about everyone in town bought land from Jackson's heirs well into the late nineteenth century.

Given the high agricultural and livestock interests of these landowners, the idea of establishing a local marketplace must have been very attractive. The building of a mill was certainly a priority (remember that Captain James Tate operated a mill before the Revolutionary War). Staunton was ten miles to the north, making access to markets selling manufactured goods tedious. The desire to develop Greenville into a "place of considerable commerce and traffic" was made clear in the trustees' original 1793 advertisement describing lots for sale. In addition to providing a marketplace for goods, another benefit of developing a town included the promise of improved transportation, as town-dwellers would share the responsibility and workload of building and maintaining new and better roads.

9

Lots Traded, Houses Built

Of particular interest to the history of my house is lot 10 on the south-side of Main Street. As described earlier, both lot 9 on the north side and lot 10 on the south side of Main Street were initially conveyed to Jacob Long on June 16, 1795, for twelve pounds. Both lots were located on street corners and presumably were desirable for their commercial value. In this regard, the river and corner lots were among the first to sell between 1794 and 1795.

Few particulars are known about Jacob Long except that he, like many original purchasers, was interested in the investment potential of Greenville. The lots he secured were not adjoining, as he did not plan to live there. Marriage records show that Long married Sarah (Sally) Burkitt, daughter of a German immigrant, Nathaniel Burkitt, on February 28, 1791, just four years before buying the two lots. Incidentally, Nathaniel Burkitt purchased lot 6 on the north side of Main Street at about the same time that Long purchased his lots; it certainly appears that the two men had common interests.

Long's investment was not profitable, and he sold both lots to David Bell one year later on June 1, 1796, for the same price he paid for the lots. Perhaps Long was in financial trouble or the town was not showing the signs of development he expected. Chancery records of 1819 and 1824 detailing Long's selling of personal property to settle debts sheds some light about his vocation and social standing. His property included: "one waggon, three bay horses, one gray mare, one iron gray colt, three milch cows, two heifers, and ten head of hogs" as well as household furnishings consisting of "a corner cubboard and four feather beds with bedsteads." These items suggest that Long was a farmer of moderate means.

More records exist to describe the new owner, David Bell. Born in September, 1755, he was the fourth son of James Bell who arrived in Augusta County from Ireland in about 1740. The Bell family settled in Long Glade near the Spring Hill community. His father was an educated man who taught school and worked as a surveyor. David Bell married Mary Christian in February, 1796, and had three children: James, John and Elizabeth.

Like Long, Bell was probably a land speculator, as he lived four miles north of Staunton. He had previously purchased 145 acres "on the waters of the South River" in 1800 plus another eighty-three acres in Augusta County in 1808. He owned land in Greenville for about eleven years, as tax and newspaper records indicate that he conveyed lot 10 to David Williams sometime between 1807 and 1808. The sale was part of an estate auction advertised in the October 9, 1807, issue of the *Staunton Eagle* which read:

On Wednesday the 28th instant, at the dwelling house of the subscriber on the Main Road to Winchester, about 4 miles from Staunton, all his personal property, consisting of a variety of household & kitchen furniture, all of a good quality — also, slaves, horses, cattle, hogs, a quantity of small grain, by the bushel, consisting of wheat, rye, corn, oats, and barley — hay, per ton, both first and second crop, with all kinds of farming utensils, one lot of ground in Greensville, and an half lot in New Haven — a riding chair & harness, and a variety of other articles too numerous to insert in this advertisement. David Bell.

The reason for this liquidation is unclear; however, the sale appears to have included all his estate except the dwelling house and land. Bell might have ventured further west as many others did during this period.

During the War of 1812, Bell distinguished himself by receiving a military commission with a rank of Captain. He went on to become a prosperous planter, leaving a fine house and farm plus four slaves when his estate was settled following his death in October, 1842. That his estate contained slaves suggests that Bell enjoyed considerable economic success. As an aside, the Bell family gained distinction for sending eighteen men into the Confederate Army during the Civil War — eleven of whom were lost.

David Williams was apparently quite interested in Greenville, as he acquired the two adjoining lots, numbers 8 and 9 on south Main Street, in 1810. No deed was ever recorded for lot 10, and no building is mentioned in the records for lots 8 and 9. The tax valuations further confirm these observations suggesting that no buildings were constructed on either lot 8, 9, or 10.

A man of some means, Williams had served in the military during the Revolutionary War and held the rank of Lieutenant when he retired from the militia in 1794. He was looking for an investment. By 1810, Greenville appeared to be a promising enterprise, as few lots remained available — even the lots on Back Street had sold quickly at twenty dollars each.

David Williams chose his investment well, as he sold his lots for a handsome profit to Joseph Huston in 1813 after only three years. The selling price was one-hundred-fifty dollars. This is the first time that premises were mentioned in a deed to this land, raising the question of whether or not a structure had been built sometime between 1807 and 1813. Given the selling price for the three lots, it does not appear that a structure was built, particularly when compared to selling prices and tax assessments of neighboring properties. Unimproved lots were valued between thirty and fifty dollars in the 1820s, the first decade that land valuations were recorded.

The new owner, Joseph Huston, was originally from Rockingham County but was listed as living in Augusta County in the 1810 US Census. He did not own land in the county before buying lots in Greenville, but he had relatives in town. His brother, Benjamin Huston, had married John Burke's daughter, Polly; Burke owned several properties in Greenville including lots numbered 6 through 9 on south Main Street and 8 and 9 on north Main Street.

On February 28, 1815, Joseph Huston bought a second property in Greenville, part of lot 4 on north Main Street, from Robert Beard. When John Burke died in 1799, he willed his six lots to his daughters Polly Huston (four lots) and Rachel Hope (two lots); however, as these families had removed to the Tennessee frontier, the lots were acquired by Joseph Huston by a deed dated May 18, 1819. This deed poses an interpretation problem, as David Williams already conveyed lots 8 and 9 on south Main Street to Huston in 1813. It is unclear whether a land transaction occurred in the interim or if a recording error occurred. In any case, Huston eventually acquired all this land.

Joseph Huston and his wife Sally sold lots 8, 9, and 10 to James Williamson five years later in 1819 for four-hundred dollars. The selling price suggests that the land was significantly improved. Huston had settled in Greenville and built a house, but the call of the frontier beckoned; the family left the region in late 1819.

James Williamson had traveled to Augusta County from Baltimore sometime before 1808. An advertisement in the January 1, 1808, issue of the *Staunton Eagle* describes him as a tailor. He brought two young apprentices with him named Elizabeth Plumer and Elizabeth Summer. His wife, Elizabeth (Hawpe), put the girls to mantua and bonnet making in Staunton. The Hawpe family had long since settled in the Greenville area; however, it is unclear whether the Williamsons actually lived there.

All told, lot 10 changed hands five times between 1794 and 1810. The parcel grew to include three consecutively numbered town lots on south Main Street at the top of the hill. A dwelling was built by Joseph Huston between 1813 and 1819, although its exact location is unclear. This progression reflected the gradual passing of lots from well-to-do farmers interested in turning a profit to residents. In addition, land values rose from six pounds or approximately twenty dollars per lot between 1794–1804 to fifty dollars per lot by 1825. Greenville was in transition, moving from its origins as a business venture toward becoming a bona fide community.

A List of the Houses & Lots in the Town of Greenville

Person Names owning Lotts	Lotts	Yearly Rent of the Lotts	Amt of Yr Taxes
Michael Apple —	1	$30	$.47
Bright John —	1	5	.8
Bell David —	1	5	.8
Doake John —	1	5	.8
Doake Robert Esq. —	1	30	.47
Feasel Michael —	1	20	.31
Finley Samuel —	2	120	1.87
Hope Nicholas —	2	20	.31
Lyons Thomas —	1	30	.47
McChesney Adam —	1	5	.8
Mitchell John —	1	5	.8
Mitchell James —	1	5	.8
Steele Robert —	1	100	1.56
Steele William Esq. —	1	100	1.56
Sholtz George —	1	30	.47
Smith Davy —	1	5	.8
Sansebough Peter —	1	15	.24
Tarbet Hugh —	1	20	.31
Williams James —	1	20	.31
Afton John —	1	20	.31
McCorgen —	1	20	.31
Guam John —	1	20	.31
Smith Christian —	1	20	.31
			$10.09

Figure 15. Greenville tax list for 1804. Greenville was listed separately on the Augusta County tax list beginning in 1801. As seen above, the columns are labeled from left to right as follows: "Person Names owning Lotts", "Lotts" (number of lots owned), "Yearly Rent of the Lotts" (refers to the value of the land plus any improvements made thereon), and "Amt of Yr Taxes" (amount of taxes owed for 1804). The tax rate was 1.56 percent that year; hence, the tax levied on unimproved lots valued at five dollars each was eight cents. Note that the most valuable improvements belonged to Samual Finley, Robert Steele, and William Steele. Also note that Thomas Lyons owned the log house situated along the north bank of the river which later became known as the second Smith Tavern. Overall, it can be seen how little many houses in Greenville were worth.

10

Prosperity Dawns

Throughout the first half of the nineteenth century, Greenville experienced a constant influx of settlers traveling along the Great Road from the north. As roads across the Blue Ridge improved, many English families from the Tidewater and Piedmont areas joined the westward movement. Still, the English represented a numerical minority compared to the Scotch-Irish and Germans, although the political trends continued to be dominated by the aristocracy in Eastern Virginia.

Contributing to the increasing numbers of settlers crossing over the Blue Ridge from the east was the building of the first graded road in Augusta County. Completed in 1827, this road ran from Staunton (along the path taken by US Route 250) to Waynesboro, going over the Blue Ridge at Rockfish Gap and continuing southeast to Scottsville via Batesville and North Garden. Established by the Staunton and James River Turnpike Company, chartered on March 8, 1824, the road provided Augusta County farmers access to the James River at Scottsville. This river town became a thriving shipping center for Augusta County goods.

Although an improvement over existing roadways, the new turnpikes of the era left much to be desired. The multiple toll gates, five in Albemarle County alone, were expensive; the one at Garland's Store near North Garden charged a wagon loaded with wheat forty-six cents per trip in 1831! In addition, the road was extremely rough and was impassable when wet with mud. Most wagons were no match for these obstacle courses; many of them simply came apart as they bounced over stone outcroppings and hardened ruts. Waddell described the roads as littered with "broken parts of wagons . . . like the debris of a battlefield." Nevertheless, the turnpike saved travelers a much longer, two-week trip to Richmond, and so was heavily used. In addition to livestock and milled products, large volumes of whiskey were shipped east, as this was an economical way to market grains. By 1810, Augusta County was producing 250,000 gallons of spirits annually, more than any other county in the Valley.

By the 1820s, the demand for commercial transportation gave rise to a booming industry. Drovers and teamsters crowded rural roadways. Traffic jams were frequent, particularly during the summer months when herds of steer, sheep, and pigs filled the road. All this traffic passed down Greenville's Main Street — an endless procession of freight wagons, horsemen, livestock, and pedestrians. Tempers flared and accidents were not uncommon, as teamsters maneuvered their heavy wagons around slower vehicles and insolent gallopers zig-zagged through the melee at break-neck speed. And as the sun set, the Smith and Finley taverns filled with rowdy teamsters, drinking and gaming while other travelers, too exhausted for revelry, tried to sleep in crowded upstairs rooms.

In addition to the mercantile traffic, many families from the north and east were passing through in a steady stream of emigration, enroute to the Tennessee Valley with their belongings piled high in sagging wagons. They were lured by the availability of land to the west just as the Scotch-Irish and Germans had come to the Greenville area some years prior. It seemed as if the entire country was migrating to the frontier. Many from well-established Valley families including the Doaks, Tates, Smiths, and Steeles joined this flow. Greenville profited from this endless stream of travelers who filled the taverns, purchased supplies, and made repairs to their wagons.

The town grew markedly during the first quarter of the

nineteenth century. Some idea of the early construction in Greenville can be gleaned from deed, tax and will records. Admittedly, many deeds did not specify if premises were included in a given conveyance and tax assessors did not reliably record lot numbers until about 1820. These problems notwithstanding, it seems clear that building activity progressed steadily during the town's first ten years.

There were at least ten houses along Main Street and six more on the Back Street in 1804. At that time, the most prominent dwellings were those of Samuel Finley, William Steele, Robert Steele, Thomas Lyons, and George Shultz. In all, twenty-five properties held among twenty-three owners were listed in 1804. Ten years later, forty-two properties held among twenty owners were listed with eighteen lots showing documented improvements. There were probably as many more buildings located just outside of town, including the *grand* homes of the aforementioned trustees.

Nearly all of these houses were of log construction with the few more valuable buildings using half-timber framing sheathed in clapboards. Many older log buildings "disappeared" under weather-boarding or were torn down. With few exceptions, the primitive structures of the earliest settlers were gone.

By 1814, Greenville was well-established as a resting place for travelers between the already prosperous towns of Staunton and Lexington. Stagecoaches traveled the Great Road as early as 1804. One of the earliest advertisements for a stage passing through Greenville appeared in the March 8, 1805, issue of the *Candid Review and Staunton Weekly Register* and read as follows:

The subscriber having contracted to run a line of stages from Staunton to Abingdon in this state begs leave to acquaint the public therewith, and solicits a share of their patronage. The stage will leave the tavern of Capt. William Chambers, in Staunton, at 2 o' clock, on the first Friday in April next, and arrive at Mr. Hay's in Wythe on the Monday evening following. — Returning — Leave Mr. Hay's on the next morning, (Tuesday) and arrive at Captain Chamber's in Staunton on the Friday morning following. Fare for passengers, six cents a mile, provided they go the whole route, with the privilege of 14 lb baggage, and eight cents a mile for way passengers. George Haller.

Abingdon was the gateway to the west, viewed by many with an air of excitement, as so many were headed in that direction. This three-day trip covered about sixty to seventy miles a day along the treacherous Great Road. Although quick for the era, stagecoach traveling was unpleasant and not for the weak of heart. Most, if not all, early coaches were without wheel springs or cushions, so the ride was as harsh and jolting as the coach's construction could bear.

Imagine a stagecoach ride: squeezed together with strangers on backless benches, a chamber pot rattling underfoot, jolting along for hours on end. If the grades were too steep, or the mud too deep, the passengers would have to walk or help push the coach along until the obstacle was passed. The only reprieve to be had was when the stagecoach stopped in towns like Greenville to rest, feed, or change the horses.

Greenville's success in catering to travelers was due to its location along several north-south routes. Three roads intersected at the north border of town connecting Greenville with Staunton, Waynesboro, and Middlebrook while the south road led to Lexington via Steeles Tavern and Fairfield. A fourth road meandered over King's Hill towards Old Providence Church, near Spotswood, and continued to the Newport-Brownsburg area.

Enticing travelers in Staunton to choose the route through Greenville was a competitive affair, as businesses located along alternative routes between Staunton and Lexington vied for a share of this traffic. The Middlebrook-Brownsburg road was a major rival for this business. This was made clear in a plea published in the November 6, 1807, issue of the *Staunton Eagle* by tavern owner Nicholas Spring declaring that:

. . . Brownsburg is twenty-two miles from Staunton, and is allowed by judges to be far the best road leading from Staunton to Lexington, and by calculation it is two miles the nearest.

In addition to being a trading hub, Greenville developed

its own industries along the South River. Since travel was so laborious, even the smallest town required access to a mill for grain, salt, linseed oil, lumber, and the like. It was not uncommon for mill sites to predate the establishing of towns, for a good mill site, regardless of how remote, was highly valued. Consequently, it would not take long for roads to find their way towards a working mill. The earliest mills known to exist in Augusta County date to the 1750s.

Although it is not known when the first mill was built in Greenville, John Tate operated a mill near town before the Revolutionary War; he continued his milling until his death in 1802. In addition, a "merchant mill" was mentioned in a deed dated 1810 for the Hessian House property, located one mile north of town along Christian's Creek. A third mill, owned by trustee James Mitchell, was located along the South River in 1819. The large stone dam for this mill was located several hundred yards west of the ford and has remained a permanent feature of the Greenville landscape throughout its history. Certainly the potential for this mill site was recognized long before the town was planned.

The miller held a high ranking among the residents of Greenville. As both a buyer and a seller of goods, the miller often set the pace for the town's economy. In Greenville, this meant the ability to transform the raw products of farm labor such as wheat, corn, and timber into marketable commodities such as flour, meal, and lumber. At the mill, prices were set, debt ledgers kept, and decisions made concerning the kinds of products produced.

Adam Hawpe, who originally purchased three-fourths of an acre across from the Smith Tavern, established a tannery along the north bank of the River as early as 1800. The size of his operation was revealed when his equipment was offered for sale in the May 3, 1805, issue of the *Candid Review and Staunton Weekly Register*:

A tan yard in the town of Greenville, Augusta County, the property of Adam Hawpe dec'd, on the main road leading from Staunton to Lexington, twelve miles from the former and twenty three from the latter, with all the implements requisite for executing the business. There are sixteen vats; two

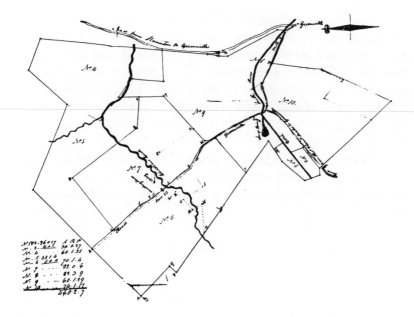

Figure 16. Lands and mill of James Mitchell, 1819. Augusta County Chancery Court records for the settlement of the James Mitchell estate in 1819 included a survey of the area northwest of Greenville. As seen above, Greenville is located in the upper right corner. The road labeled, "Road from Staunton to Greenville" is the Old Greenville Road (Virginia routes 613 and 1206); the second road running through the center of the map is the Middlebrook Road (Virginia Route 662 West). The mill site is located near the current mill dam on the south side of the river.

slimes; two handlers, one bait and one pool included in the number. Terms will be ascertained by applying to the subscribers, one living in Greenville, the other one mile distant. Catherine Hawpe, John Hawpe.

John Hawpe later operated a sawmill in the 1840s located just east of the town along the South River. Its production would later stimulate the use of frame construction in Greenville.

On balance, the town was indeed well-situated for commerce, travel, and industry, as the trustees had predicted twenty years earlier. But one wonders what it was like to live in Greenville in the period between 1800 and 1830. It is tempting to romanticize about how Greenville might have looked back then; however, it is likely that our modern sensibilities would be shocked by what we would see.

Along the River, the sights, sounds, and smells were of a busy industry. The tannery, with its smoking vats filling the air with a burnt odor, appeared as a cluttered lot with wood piles on one end and work sheds on the other. The fire pits burned close to the river so the vats could be easily filled. The river itself was littered with debris. In the distance, the mill ground along, a rhythmic creaking of wood heard over the distant roar of water pouring over the wheel. Droves of cattle and a near continuous procession of wagons and horses added to the commercial din of the Main Street landscape.

The street was muddy enough to swallow a man's boots when wet and extremely dusty in the hot summer sun. Huge, wheel-breaking ruts scarred the road in many places. Few, if any, houses had grass, shrubs, or shade trees, as most were built directly on the street. Paint was generally unavailable such that boards and logs weathered to a grey-brown. Upkeep on dwellings was poor; broken windows were rudely patched, warped doors remained so, and roofs leaked. Dust routinely drifted indoors, and in the summer, swarms of flies were commonplace.

The house yard was typically viewed as a functional area to keep domestic animals including hogs and chickens. Trash was often pitched out of windows with abandon. Litter in the form of decaying food, wood chips, and animal dung was everywhere; the stench could be heavy at times. Smoke filled the air from chimneys. Waddell noted the lack of concern for the domestic environment in the 1830s, even in Staunton where conditions might be expected to be more improved:

> . . . no pavement or sidewalk existed on Fredrick Street from end to end. People walking shared the way with horses and cows, all alike trampling through the mud and mire. Moreover, there were several stables immediately on that and other streets, and piles of litter thrown out on the highway adorned every stable door, and sent their fetid drainage meandering through the gutters of the town. Many dwelling houses were on Fredrick, and the inmates, whenever they went out, had to pass over or around the obstructions mentioned as best they could. In rainy weather,

the ground around the courthouse yard was like a swamp.

And so it was in Greenville. It was not until the 1850s that sanitary and cosmetic concerns for the landscape began to take shape. As this transition occurred, garbage pits were dug, fences built to enclose some parts of yards, and whitewash became popular for house exteriors. Yet, we yearn for the "good olde days . . . "

11

A Grand House is Built

We return our attention to lot 10 on the south side of Main Street. Having purchased lots 8, 9, and 10 from Joseph Huston in 1819 for four-hundred dollars, James Williamson and his wife owned property in Greenville for only four years before selling the property, plus lot 7, to brothers Robert and Thomas Steele for five-hundred-twenty dollars in 1822. Since a single house was mentioned in this transaction, the increase in selling price between 1819 and 1822 was probably due to the added lot plus an overall increase in land values. It is likely that the house mentioned in the 1822 document was the same structure referred to in 1819. Later deeds suggest that this house was located on lot 7 or 8.

The 1822 deed also suggests that much of south Main Street above lot 8 was flanked by vacant lots. This was not unusual since the early buildings in Greenville were concentrated, for the sake of convenience, along the South River. Nevertheless, later deeds and tax assessments indicated an increase in building activity on many lots located away from the river in the period that immediately followed.

Robert Steele was an integral part of this development. Born in 1787 to original Greenville founders Thomas and Jane Steele, he was thirty-five years old in 1822 and already a promising entrepreneur. He married Mary Steele on December 20, 1812, and according to family history, married twice more, although the names of these wives are unknown. His business relation to Thomas Steele (named on the deed) is unclear, although the two shared ownership of several properties in Rockbridge County.

Information about Robert Steele's business activities comes from a series of liquidations which occurred throughout 1837 and 1838, recorded in deed and will records. He conducted business on a grand scale, which included partnerships in all the neighboring counties and as far away as Delaware, Pennsylvania, and Missouri. "Mercantile concerns" represented a large portion of his business in Augusta, Bath, Rockbridge, and Pocahontas counties. Certainly, he was a well-traveled man. In addition, he held interest in patent rights for an apple mill, a threshing machine, and a spring saddle. This new and improved saddle was developed in Greenville, as we shall see later. Despite these wide-ranging responsibilities, Robert Steele had much to contend with at home. He not only owned a store located on Main Street, but also ran a busy livestock-trading business in town.

In addition to his business concerns, Robert Steele was very active in the community and was one of the contributors to the founding of a Greenville school in 1822. In March, 1836, he conveyed lot 14 on south Main Street to trustees Henry Beard, William Clarke, John Anderson, Henry Markwood, and John Leash to build "thereon a place or house of worship for the use of the members of the Methodist Episcopal Church."

Robert Steele and his family probably lived in one of several houses located along Greenville's Main Street. He was the original purchaser of lot 4 on south Main Street in 1795; tax records indicate building improvements as early as 1801. He might also have lived in the house previously occupied by James Williamson between 1822 and 1829. Given his business successes, it is not surprising that Robert Steele eventually chose to build a new house of brick and of the latest style. This house was located on lot 10, on the corner of Main and Crofs streets.

A digression is needed here to pinpoint the year of the house's construction. Since the deed records are sketchy in their descriptions and combine lots 7 through 10, these records had to be interpreted with the tax records to determine the date of construction. Between 1829 and 1830, the tax records showed $1460 in improvements on lots 8 through 10. This tax valuation increased to $1800 in 1835 accompanied by the notation "new improvements." The building or addition referred to by this added $340 improvement is unspecified. The next conveyance of lots 8 through 10, dated May, 1836, specifically mentioned "a house and lots" which sold for $2500. Finally, lot 10 is isolated in a third conveyance dated 1839 (described in a notation in the tax records) which revealed a building valued at seven-hundred dollars. This value suggests that the house was included in the initial improvements begun in 1829.

One final piece of corroborating evidence that Robert Steele built the house comes from a more recent source provided by Brake. In a letter dated September 3, 1931, written by Virginia Bray to Leona Houser Effenger, a reference to a house in Greenville is provided as follows:

Our grandfather was . . . James Wendel Steele and lived at the old Steele place owned by my father. The old house stood there many years just as he left it — my sisters and I sold it to Roy Hanger after my mother's death and it at that time, had belonged to the Steeles for over one hundred and fifty years —of course, that was only a very small part of the estate.

As we shall see, Roy and Olivia Hanger lived in the house between 1902 and 1957; it was the only house they ever owned. Although the assumption that the house remained in the Steele family since 1829 is inaccurate, the labeling of the house as the "old Steele place" is supported by tax and deed records. No other record of James Wendel Steele having lived there exists.

12

High Style Construction

Brick construction was rapidly gaining popularity in the upper Valley during the first quarter of the nineteenth century. In his *History* of the lower Valley, Samuel Kercheval noted that the first brick house west of the Blue Ridge was built in 1785 by John Hite of Rockingham County. This date is perhaps too late to characterize the use of brick in the upper Valley, as brick was available as early as 1760–1762 when the Anglican Church was constructed in Staunton. However, brick did not see wide use for private dwellings in Augusta County until after the American Revolution; some of the earliest upper Valley houses constructed of brick include Walnut Grove built outside of Waynesboro before 1800 and the George Campbell House built about 1782 just south of the Augusta County line near Raphine.

Brick construction in Greenville appears to have occurred within the narrow time-span of 1829 to 1840 and is represented by five buildings of which only three still exist: the Steele House, the Breckenridge-Vines House, and the rear ells of the Smith Tavern. The original Methodist Church built in 1836 was constructed of brick and a schoolhouse located on Jack's Hill was described as a masonry building. Both structures are gone. Old brick chimneys can be found on several other log/frame buildings including the Apple House. Brake has suggested that a brickyard was located on the site of the present Greenville car-wash, as a surprising number of bricks were unearthed there. It is also likely that temporary kilns were set up on the house lots where the construction took place.

Although the bricks from each of the three surviving structures are of roughly the same dimensions, this is inconclusive evidence for a common origin, as early brick dimensions across all of Virginia show little variation. Rather, brick sizes were primarily determined by the amount of clay a brickmaker could comfortably throw into a mold and was shaped less by any local variations.

Much attention was given to the facade of the Steele House, as the bricks were laid in a decorative pattern where stretchers alternated with headers along the front and north walls — a popular nineteenth century pattern known as Flemish bond. Since much of Greenville was located down the hill to the north, this decorative pattern was chosen only for the sides of the house presented to the public; the rear and south walls were bricked in the less-decorative, easier to lay, three-course American bond. Traces of red paint and chalked mortar joints suggest that the decorative bond was further highlighted to produce a sharp, uniform appearance not readily achieved using hand-made bricks —this too was a common practice for high-style houses. In addition, the north chimney was decoratively corbeled at the top, whereas the southside chimney was built square and unadorned. Finally, the facade was decorated with a molded brick cornice.

This latter design feature — the molded cornice — deserves additional mention, as it represents a local building tradition frequently found in upper Valley masonry houses built between 1810 and 1859. The use of specially shaped bricks required additional effort by the mason to choose and align them properly. The shape of the curve is termed a *cyma recta* and represents a dominant element of the Federal style which was popular at the time. The use of both Flemish and American bonds as well as the molded brick cornice is also found on the other brick buildings in Greenville.

The dimensions of the Steele House are can be understood in terms of its geometric organization. The geometric principles employed were considered part of the acumen of any

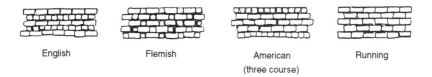

English   Flemish   American   Running
                         (three course)

Figure 17. Masonry details found in Greenville. As seen in the illustrations above, three kinds of masonry bonds were used in the construction of houses found in Greenville. The oldest bond is English Bond and its exclusive use can be found in very early brick houses dating back to the first quarter of the eighteenth century; most of these structures are located in Tidewater, Virginia. Although English Bond is some twelve percent stronger than Flemish Bond, the latter bond became popular in the early nineteenth century, especially in the Valley, for its decorative impact. Three, five, or seven course American Bond was used in Virginia after 1780 and was considered comparable to English Bond in its strength. The three brick Greenville houses of this era show Flemish Bond on the front and one side, whereas American Bond was used on the rear. The early masonry chimneys on the Apple House and the Thomas McKirgan House used Running Bond. The molded brick cornice pictured above was also a very popular decorative design element on upper Valley houses from about 1810 to the Civil War; a VHLC survey of antebellum brick houses revealed that as many as sixty percent had molded brick cornices.

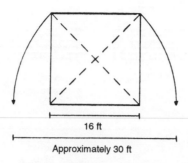

16 ft

Approximately 30 ft

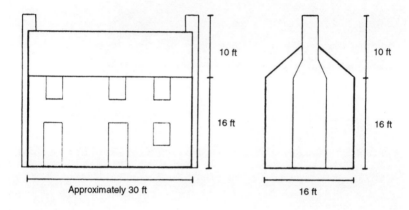

10 ft

16 ft

Approximately 30 ft

10 ft

16 ft

16 ft

Figure 18. Geometric organization of the Robert Steele House. The builder employed a 16-foot square as the basic unit for designing the Robert Steele House. Using stakes, string, and a measuring rod, the square was centered on the building site, then the diagonals of the square were rotated to each side to produce a rectangle measuring approximately 16 feet by 30 feet. This geometric manipulation of the square has a long architectural history and was used by builders in designing many sixteenth- and seventeenth-century Welsh and English houses. The 16-foot length of the square has its roots in early medieval building codes; it has been suggested by some historians that this length was the minimum needed to allow two oxen to stand side-by-side in a single bay. The elevation of the Robert Steele House was made equal to this width (16 feet), thereby keeping the overall dimensions of the building few and simple. The roof pitch and chimney height were designed such that the proportion between the total elevation and the elevation of the facade produced the Golden Section — a ratio of 1:1.6. This ratio dates to antiquity and was considered innately pleasing to look at. In summary, the dimensions of the Robert Steele House reflect a practical approach to design, economy of form, and a deliberate use of aesthetic principles.

accomplished builder and were based upon a long building tradition. These principles shared both aesthetic and practical importance. On the one hand, they involved the use of proportional systems that were considered "pleasing to the eye." On the other hand, they allowed the builder to estimate the amount of bricks and timbers needed to complete the house. In addition, geometric principles could be readily manipulated using the surveying instruments of the period (e.g., a measuring rod, square, plumb bob, level, string, and stakes).

In the Steele House, the length of the facade is twice its depth (16 by 30 feet) and twice its elevation from foundation to cornice (16 by 30 feet). Consequently, each side wall forms a perfect square (16 by 16 feet). The relationship between the facade height (16 feet) and the overall elevation from chimney top to foundation (26 feet) produces a ratio of 1:1.6. This ratio (also known as the "Golden Section") is thought to possess natural beauty and has a long architectural history dating to antiquity. These dimensions follow a simple geometric plan which manipulates a 16 by 16 foot square to produce a house of the desired proportions.

The fenestration of the Steele House was patterned after the progressive house styles in vogue throughout the upper Valley. The ideal house had a three-bay, symmetrically organized facade. As mentioned before, the emerging Georgian style placed a high premium upon balanced house design. But here, the Steele House exhibits a deviation: the facade is not symmetrical. Despite maintaining the *correct* number of openings on the second floor, the fenestration appears stretched. In addition, the first floor had two doorways: one to the far left (north end) and a second doorway to the middle right (south end). The builder conformed to the Georgian model by breaking it down into fractional components: the south half of the facade reflected the more recognizable fenestration of the ideal model (two-thirds of a three-bay Georgian design), whereas the north end fenestration simply aligned the doorway and window in the same bay.

If the fenestration found on the Steele House was unique, then it would be easy to consider this deviation from the

Figure 19. Original fenestration of the Robert Steele House, circa 1829. The Robert Steele House originally had two front doors: the left one opened into a 13-by-16-foot parlor, whereas the right one opened into a 17-by-16-foot hall. The actual use of the parlor can only be guessed at; it might have functioned as either a formal space for entertaining and business dealings or as a master bedchamber. The overall fenestration is composed of two separate Georgian elements as indicated by the dividing line pictured above — a two-thirds design on the right, and a single bay on the left. The two design elements were added together such that the distance between the left window and the left wall (3.5 feet) and the distance between the two right-side windows (5 feet) was used to determine the dividing line between the two elements. Hence, the dividing line is located 3.5 feet from the left window and 5 feet from the right window; not surprisingly, the single bay on the left makes-up exactly one-third of the facade (10 feet). The builder employed a complex model of symmetry whereby each design element, left and right, was centered with respect to the outside walls and the dividing line. The photograph, below the diagram, shows the rear ell of the Smith Tavern; this ell evidences a similar fenestration (in reverse) as the original Robert Steele House.

Georgian model as a lone idiosyncrasy; however, many Augusta County houses show similar deviations. In fact, the ell on the Smith Tavern has a similar fenestration. This suggests that the process of adapting to the new Georgian house form did not involve a rigid adherence to a single prototypical pattern (i.e., a symmetrical facade with a center hall floorplan), but rather involved the addition and subtraction of Georgian design concepts to fit older floorplans. This flexibility in design is analogous to the process of forming new sentences from relatively fixed grammatical rules. The rules for building Georgian houses, although not written down, were quite specific and included relatively fixed ideas about balance, symmetry, and the relationships among doors and windows; however, these rules could be combined in novel ways.

One is prompted to question why the full Georgian model with its premium upon style was not built in its entirety or in perfect fractional parts (as was done when constructing the Apple House). The answer lies somewhere between the desire for external symmetry and balance versus a reluctance to abandon the traditional, hall-and-parlor floorplan with two front doors. The latter floorplan with its unequal room sizes was so familiar to the Scotch-Irish way of life that it was hard to abandon. This conflict was psychological, as it marked a balancing of Old World ideals with multicultural conformity. It was a conflict not to be resolved quickly, and as a result, traditional floorplans lagged behind changing external styles. In the Steele House, it manifested in a somewhat complicated facade.

In contrast, a model which accommodated the hall-and-parlor floorplan, but made fewer pretensions towards a three-bay design, was evidenced on the original Breckenridge-Vines House facade. External symmetry was achieved by using a four-bay design which placed two front doors side-by-side allowing the second-floor windows to be placed in direct alignment above the first floor openings. One door led to the hall, and the other led to the parlor. This fenestration also satisfied the desire for a balanced, symmetrical facade. The

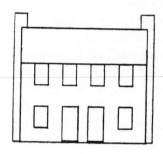

Figure 20. Original fenestration of the Breckenridge-Vines House, circa
1836. The fenestration of this hall and parlor house once had two front
doors as pictured above. Each door led to a separate room. The hall was
located on the left side and the parlor was to the right; the rooms were of
equal size. Although an older four-bay fenestration was used, the design
achieved one of the more important Georgian ideals — namely, a perfectly
balanced and symmetrical facade.

brick half of the Breckenridge-Vines House was built on half of lot 3, north Main Street, around 1836.

The two front doors is a design element more common among acculturated German houses in Pennsylvania and Maryland but is frequently encountered in the Valley. Some historians believe that this characteristic predated acceptance of the center hall floorplan and allowed for more control over traffic to either the hall or parlor. For example, family members would routinely use the hall doorway in the course of day-to-day activities and chores, whereas the parlor doorway was reserved for entertaining guests. This arrangement also protected the guests from having to pass through the rudeness of the hall to get to the parlor. The doors have been variously called the "front door" and the "very front door" to reflect this social practice.

Some oral histories refer to a "marrying," or alternatively, a "burying" door. As the stories go, newly married couples would enter the house for the first time through the marrying door and never use it again until one of them was brought out in a coffin! The second door was used for all the comings and goings in between. The validity of these tales notwithstanding, a common part of nearly all these explanations is the observation that the parlor door was rarely used. House historians have frequently remarked that the parlor door can be identified nowadays because it is the one that lacks a screen door. Perhaps Robert Steele's entrepreneurial activities demanded that he have a separate entrance to the parlor. One thing is for sure, the parlor door was considered important enough to compromise adherence to the ideal Georgian model.

Returning our attention to the interior of the Steele House, the sixteen-inch masonry walls were directly plastered with a mixture of lime and sand with animal hair added for tensile strength. The right front door opened into the hall; this was the larger of the two first-floor rooms and measured 17 feet long by 16 feet wide. The parlor, separated from the hall by a beaded board wall on the left, measured 13 feet long by 16 feet wide. A narrow staircase, running along the board wall, was located in the left-rear corner of the hall, whereas a rear door was located near the opposite corner.

Both first-floor rooms and the south second-floor room are served with fireplaces; it is unclear why the fourth room was left unheated. The downstairs mantels are substantial, both measuring sixty-three inches tall. A widely published carpenter's guide to mantel designs by Robert Adams was influential at the time, but as several historians have commented, Valley craftsmen took particular pride in their utilization of unique designs which often stood taller and had more elaborate embellishments than those found in the published guides. This attention to detail reflected the prominence that the hearth held as the center of activity, especially during the colder months. As such, the mantel represented the dominant decorative feature in most rooms.

A specialized vocabulary is needed to describe the design elements of a mantel. The basic pattern defining an Adams or Federal mantel includes two supporting half-columns (pilasters) upon which rests a broad crossmember (lintel) framed by end-blocks. The frieze refers to the flat portion of the lintel just below the cornice and typically consists of panels adorned with decorative moldings. As seen in the photographs, the mantels inside the Steele House are every bit as elaborate as the decorative masonry outside. The first-floor parlor mantel exhibits fluted pilasters, cyma molded cornices and a two-panel frieze; this is the better of the three mantels. The mantel in the hall, while similar in size and construction, is framed with elaborate moldings instead of pilasters and appears less formal; this mantel, due to its lack of pilasters, represents an older design. The second-floor mantel is much simpler with unadorned pilasters and solid block frieze.

Window, door, and floor moldings all have a single bead along the inside edge with the doorway also displaying an attached ovolo (quarter-round) molding along the outside edge. The single bead is continued on the outer edge of each vertical wall board — a style frequently seen in Valley houses, dating as early as the 1750s. The floors were finished with tongue-and-groove heart pine ranging between four and six

Figure 21. Federal style mantels in the Robert Steele House, circa 1829. The parlor mantel pictured on top measures 63 inches tall and 80 inches across; hence, it covers nearly half the wall and is a dominant feature of the room. The hall mantel pictured on the bottom shares the same dimensions but is less ornate.

inches in width. Four panel doors and six-pane over six-pane window sash were used for the openings.

The Steele House is built on the edge of a hill. A dry-laid limestone foundation follows the contour of the ground and permits a cellar entrance under the northern (i.e., downhill) front of the house. This cellar was never used as a utility or cooking space, but did provide cold storage. The roof is simply framed using sets of rafters lap-jointed and pegged together without a ridge pole and was originally sheathed with wooden shingles which appear in early twentieth-century photographs.

13

Unconscious Influences

The house that Robert Steele built represented a transitional style — one caught between a desire to project the Georgian ideal of balanced design on the outside while maintaining traditional patterns of living on the inside. The house stood as a symbol of Steele's social and business success, traits reflected through its contemporary style and brick construction. Two full stories, gable end chimneys, decorative Flemish bond with molded cornice bricks, and a balanced facade were all well-recognized features of the homes that the gentry were building. Along with the Apple and Breckenridge-Vines houses, the Steele House was probably one of the grandest in Greenville at the time.

To appreciate the symbolic importance of this brick house in 1829, the climate of acculturation must be understood. As mentioned before, early building occurred in a context of ethnic optimism tempered with a press to satisfy functional demands. Old World designs that provided familiar living spaces dominated building plans. Yet, as the German and Scotch-Irish cultures clashed with those of the English gentry, and as the Valley wilderness became tamed, the old designs became less fashionable. Current fashion, and the status it brought, were becoming more important. As such, old house designs gave way to a more amalgamated, uniquely American interpretation of English building styles. The Georgian house became a social statement with old ways of organizing floorspace hidden on the inside behind a status-seeking facade. This revolution in design stemmed from several factors.

Despite representing a numerical minority, land owner-ship and political power in the Valley was largely controlled by the English gentry. Ethnic tolerance among the English was dictated more by politics than by any real effort to wel-come or accept the Germans and Scotch-Irish. Their overrid-ing concern was the rapid population of the Valley to estab-lish a buffer zone between the Piedmont and the French-and-Indian West. Similarly, multicultural heterogeneity was tolerated by land grant holders, like William Beverley, due to their own economic yearnings — simply put, they sold land for personal profit and did not care who they were selling it to.

The political advantages long held by the English had a pervasive impact upon cultural expression in everyday life. Both the Germans and Scotch-Irish were disliked, and their cultural expressiveness was openly criticized, by the English. These sentiments, coupled with fears of an uprising, were articulated by Virginia Governor Robert Dinwiddle in the 1750s when he wrote:

> The Germans in Pennsyl'a live all in a body together, as if in a principality of Germany, may they not in time throw off their obedience and submission to the British crown? It was, I think, a very imprudent step in the first settlem't of y't province not to mix them in their settlem'ts with the Eng., and have English school masters & c. Whereas there are now many thousands cannot speak one word of English.

The Scotch-Irish, too, were subjected to intense scorn from the English. One English observer described them as "to the last degree, unclenly and unwholesome and discusting."

In addition to English prejudice, the Germans and Scotch-Irish had to contend with each other, for as the Valley became more and more populated, it was increasingly difficult to live separately, worship separately, form separate communities, and so on. These clashes worked against open cultural expres-sion. Consequently, there came to be a strong press for meld-ing ethnic traditions towards a more commonly held, American tradition.

This melding of traditions included building practices. Old World designs with their odd placements of windows and off-center chimneys were replaced with a design that was neither German nor Scotch-Irish. Yet during this transition period, patterns of living and organizing space, as evidenced by floorplan design, remained unchanged, such that houses became less culturally-typed on the outside only. External architectural detailing served to give the public the impression of multicultural conformity.

The Georgian model was not only revered for its geometrically balanced facade, but it also had associations with English society, and like military titles, the English social order was something that prosperous Valley planters wanted to emulate. As might be expected, high-style houses built by the more affluent Germans and Scotch-Irish began to resemble the traditional, classically-influenced, English house — tall, rectangular, with twin gable-end chimneys.

A second and interrelated trend stemming from the frontier experience itself also influenced building styles. Confronted with the formidable task of establishing new lives on the frontier, the settlers in the Valley were shaped by a number of common psychological influences. The deeply ingrained human need to create order out of chaos governed the evolution of a mind-set which placed high value on the use of man-made construction materials. Such materials symbolized the taming of the wilderness. A house of logs was viewed as a temporary shelter at best, whereas a house of planed boards or bricks was considered permanent. This ethic was underscored in the tax valuations for Greenville: frame houses, like the one Samuel Finley built, were highly valued and were insured as such, whereas log structures, even large ones, were worth less.

The press to transform naturally-found building materials into man-made products echoed the challenge of creating a new societal order in the New World. As settlement of the Valley progressed, so too did the shaping of *acceptable* building materials. Initially, houses were built with raw materials such as coarse stone and logs, but as the Valley peoples became more secure, building materials such as thinly planed weather-boarding and brick came into vogue, particularly among the gentry. Even the farmer of meager means sheathed his house of logs with clapboarding as soon as he could afford to. In this context, it was only a matter of time before brick would become the building material of choice. Even the use of stone, often reserved only for chimneys, was discarded whenever brick became available, even if only the top of the chimney (i.e., the most visible part) was the only portion bricked.

In an instance of philosophical editorializing, Peyton expounded upon the virtues of building a solid house. He wrote:

> . . . fine private mansions and public edifices imply the evolution of a highly organized man brought to supreme delicacy of sentiment; are the evidences of an advancing on an advanced civilization, and of the growth of a nation after its own genius.
>
> . . . the effect of a brick or stone house is immense on the tranquillity, power and refinement of the builder. A man in a cave or in a camp, a nomad, will die with no more estate than the wolf or horse leaves. But so simple a labor as a house being achieved, his chief enemies are kept at bay. He is safe from the teeth of wild animals, from frost, sunstroke and weather, and fine faculties begin to yield their rich harvest; invention and art are born, manners and social beauty and delight. The builders of these durable edifices belong to the class of men who have left the world better than they found it . . .

Peyton's powerful sentiment counted the building of substantial houses among the highest of societal values.

Together, these unconscious influences helped shape the house that Robert Steele built. It represented the emerging Valley style: an English-influenced hall-and-parlor floorplan, with two gable-end chimneys. The fenestration was near symmetrical despite unequal room sizes inside. It was constructed entirely of brick, laid in decorative Flemish-bond on both the front and north sides — where the public could see. The elaborate molded cornice bricks became a standard mark of style in the upper Valley. Overall, the house represented a new American ethic — a symbol of both material success and psychological stability.

The strength of these unconscious yearnings revealed itself in the decade that followed (1830–1840), as the Valley witnessed a most remarkable building spurt in American architectural history. Hundreds of houses were built in the Georgian style; previous building styles all but disappeared. The Valley and its people were coming of age.

Quite by historical accident, this vernacular house style was identified as a mid-western type in the 1930s and was labeled by architectural historians as the "I-house." The "I" stands for Iowa, Illinois, and Indiana, places where this two-story, one-room deep, two-rooms wide, gable-end form was first widely studied. It was recognized that the design had *migrated* from Pennsylvania and the Virginia Valley to the upland south and midwest where, there too, it became a symbol of economic attainment among the rural aristocracy.

14

Business Dealings

Robert Steele suffered major financial problems beginning in the mid-1830s. The whole country was experiencing an economic depression. In reaction to his financial difficulties, Robert Steele appointed Greenville entrepreneur John Newton to auction off his assets. Considerable acreage around Greenville and in Rockbridge County as well as cattle, slaves, and household items were sold in this manner. Robert Steele subsequently left Virginia and settled in Missouri.

John Newton was the right man for the job, as he was in the business of liquidating estates as well as sponsoring large slave auctions. As a result, he amassed a considerable fortune which included many properties in Greenville. Following his death in 1869, his sons, John and Isaac, carried on his business dealings well into the 1880s. In particular, Isaac practiced law in Greenville and Staunton; his estate included several dwelling houses, a tanyard, and the Greenville Hotel (formerly Samuel Finley's tavern).

John Newton sold the house and lots 8, 9, and part of lot 10 (on which the house stands) in May, 1836, for the princely sum of $2500 to George B. and John A. Tate. No other buildings were mentioned in this conveyance but it might also be the case that commercial buildings were not explicitly mentioned in the conveyance, as the selling price was excessive for the property listed. In addition, only "part of lot ten" was sold. According to tax records, Robert Steele did not lose money on the sale, as the 1838 property valuation was $1800 for improvements and one-hundred dollars for land.

George B. and John A. Tate, the new owners, were brothers whose great uncle was the Valley patriot Captain James Tate. They both were prominent men of an esteemed family who lived outside Greenville. The Steele properties were probably bought for resale. Between 1838 and 1839, tax records indicate that the house was conveyed to Harvey and Lucy Beard (no deed was recorded) who then sold the house, plus an adjoining parcel of land behind the lot, to their son, Anthony Beard (aged thirty-seven) in 1841 for eight-hundred dollars. In all, the property contained one acre, two rods, and thirty-five poles. The additional land was located behind the town lots and was probably used for family farming; no buildings are known to have been built there. At that time, the house was assessed to be worth seven-hundred-fifty dollars plus fifty dollars land value.

Anthony and his wife, Martha (Brand), had married five years earlier in February of 1836; the opportunity to move into a new brick house in the center of town must have been an exciting event. They lived there fifteen years and raised a large family. The 1850 census indicated that Anthony and Martha then had six children: Mary (thirteen years), John (ten years), David (ten years), John (seven years), Rebecca (four years), and Martha (one year). In addition, a grandmother or aunt named Rebecca Beard (eighty-five years) lived with the family.

The Beard family was descendent from William Beard who established a successful plantation near New Hope around 1784. His grandson, Thomas Beard, moved to the Riverheads area in the early 1800s and was well-respected in Greenville. At one time, he owned several lots on Main Street. It is not clear how he is related to Harvey Beard who purchased part of lot 3 on south Main Street in 1833 and lot 8 on north Main Street in 1839. Harvey had also purchased twelve acres (in two parcels) bordering Greenville from William Jackson in 1839.

Harvey Beard and his son were in business together during the mid-1830s and sold patent rights for their "Zig-zag or U-shaped steel-spring seat saddle, spring girth and iron horn." This invention was described as involving a "new and useful improvement in the mode of making and manufacturing saddles." On September 26, 1835, Robert Steele and Alexander McClure purchased the "exclusive right and liberty of making, constructing, using and vending" this invention within the state of Pennsylvania as well as within Brook and Ohio counties in Virginia. A term of fourteen years was allowed although the purchase price for these rights was not given. A similar deal was made with Thomas Jackson (of Greenville) and was limited to the state of Missouri. The Beards' invention was probably developed in Greenville since the marketing rights were sold only to local entrepreneurs.

There were several shops manufacturing saddles and wagon equipment on Main Street including a blacksmithing shop located directly across the street. It is likely that the Beards' shop was located on one of the aforementioned lots owned by Harvey Beard. In addition, the 1850 census revealed that Anthony Beard boarded an eighteen year-old saddler's apprentice named James Hall. Together, these tradesmen worked to outfit horses and wagons for use in the great westward movement through Kentucky and Tennessee in the 1840s and 1850s.

It is noteworthy that the manufacture of leather ranked among the largest industries in the upper Valley by 1800. Nearly every town had its own tannery. Augusta County was Virginia's leading producer of saddleware during the first half of the nineteenth century. Such was the demand for a country in motion.

15

Changing Floorplans

Much of what is known about patterns of domestic living during the first half of the nineteenth century has been derived from the study of floorplans. Examining room arrangements not only reveals clues about how people organized their living space, but also reflects broader cultural, social, and economic factors which influenced how people lived day-to-day. As the exterior of the Steele House publicly proclaimed membership in the emerging American culture, the interior shaped family life.

In the hall-and-parlor house, the hall represented the focus of domestic activity. A multi-purpose living space, this was where the family prepared food, cooked, dined, and socialized. Personal privacy was not a prominent feature of many early hall-and-parlor houses, as frontier families typically lived in a more communal fashion. In the early days, it was not unusual for family members to share the same eating utensils. The parlor was often unheated and used for storage and sleeping.

The Steele House resembled these early hall-and-parlor houses in design only, as patterns of living were rapidly changing. It is likely that the domestic activities involving food preparation and cooking were confined to a detached kitchen, whereas the larger hall evolved into a dining room. The parlor, too, was elevated in status, for it was heated and boasted a fine mantel; it was very likely used for family gatherings and/or as a master bed chamber. Consequently, the hall-and-parlor floorplan in the Steele House was already outdated when the house was built, yet it was chosen because it was familiar.

These new uses of traditional spaces reflected a trend experienced throughout American households which began to take shape as early as 1700 along the eastern seaboard and was only now appearing in Valley homes fifty to one-hundred years later. This transition was marked by a growing distinction between social and utilitarian uses of domestic space. Put another way, formal versus informal rooms were becoming a defining characteristic in architecture. That social formality and personal space was becoming more important in the mid-1700s has been evidenced in archaeological findings throughout Virginia, revealing a sudden and four-fold increase in the use of specific-purpose plates, glasses, and utensils; dining was becoming less of an intimate affair and more of a social event by the 1750s. Similarly, the diversity and decorativeness of dinnerware rapidly became a symbol of gentility.

The hall became associated with formal dining while the domestic chores associated with meals were moved to less public areas — that is, pushed back to detached kitchens and rear ells or pushed down to basements. This division between cooking and living spaces is considered by many to reflect a growing awareness of social class; increasingly, landlords strove to differentiate themselves from activities of servants or slaves. The hall became the "company" room, richly decorated and ceremonial in function. Impressing visitors became all-important.

As social function gained prominence in domestic life, a physical transformation in floorplans began to emerge in the form of the central passageway. As mentioned earlier, the central passageway was part of the Georgian house plan, but it was not until the first quarter of the nineteenth century that this floorplan gained wide acceptance in the Valley. This modification brought both formality and privacy to the house, as it controlled traffic flow in ways that were impossible in the earlier hall-and-parlor houses. Access to either the hall or the parlor was now selective; consequently, the center passage was used as a waiting area to greet visitors before inviting or not inviting them to enter either of the two heated rooms. In this way, visitors of lower social standing could be dealt with in the passageway, whereas important guests could be honored with an invitation to enter the hall or parlor. In contrast to houses with two front doors, the central passageway eliminated the confusion that often resulted when visitors tried to guess which door to knock on.

In addition to meeting both social and privacy needs, the emergence of the central passage paved the way for the further adoption of the highly-prized Georgian ideal. The passageway provided a focus around which to organize rooms, particularly in the expanded two-room deep houses that became popular in the upper Valley after 1850. On the outside, the central passage design lent itself to the perfectly balanced, symmetrical facade which rapidly became the norm for Valley houses built after 1830. Similarly, the central passage allowed the one-room deep I-house to be considered a variant of the full Georgian model: it was a one-half Georgian design (i.e., the front half). This added respectability insured that the I-house form would continue to dominate the Valley landscape until the 1920s.

By the 1840s, the I-house with a central hall was assimilated into the repertoire of Valley builders; nearly every house built in Greenville between 1835 and 1870 represented some variant of this model. On Main Street, this central passage plan was exemplified by the James Mitchell House located on lot 8 directly across from the Steele House. This antebellum house was built of wood-pegged, half-timber framing with brick infill. The facade was perfectly symmetrical with a three-bay fenestration. Inside, two beaded board walls defined a narrow central passage on both floors with an enclosed staircase along the left side of the hallway.

Given the many advantages of the central passage floorplan, it is not surprising that Anthony Beard added a central hallway to the Steele House sometime during the 1840s. A frame and plaster wall partitioned off a seven-foot passage from the hall. A similar modification was made by

Figure 22. James Mitchell House, circa 1830–1860. This house represents a prototypical Virginia Valley I-house with its symmetrical, three-bay facade on the outside and a central passageway on the inside. Gable-end chimneys on antebellum I-houses were the norm, whereas paired internal chimneys located along either side of the central passageway were the fashion in the 1870s and later. In addition, many post-Civil War I-houses had a decorative center gable added to the facade.

adding a second vertical board wall upstairs, creating a small second-floor landing. These modifications were probably considered necessary given his large family of nine children.

It is likely that the parlor front door was bricked-up at this time. In addition, a window was added to the left of the hall doorway in order to provide light for the parlor. These modifications brought the house as close to the three-bay Georgian ideal as possible. Overall, the I-house configuration was satisfied in three ways: 1) the first floor fenestration taken by itself (a single door centered between two windows), 2) the unaltered right half of the facade (representing a perfect two-thirds of the ideal model), and 3) the correct number of windows (but not equally spaced) on the second floor. These modifications to the floorplan and facade of the Steele House illustrate the pervasiveness of the Georgian ideal in the Valley.

The Beards added a lateral frame addition to the southern end of the house. This demand for more space echoed a trend in enlarging I-houses with either the addition of a rear ell, running perpendicular to the main house, or the addition of a lateral extension. The latter kind of addition was less common. One reason Anthony Beard might have decided to build a lateral addition was because the rising terrain along the back of the house made a rear ell more expensive. The site of this lateral addition is where the Steeles' detached kitchen most likely stood, as it was easily accessible from both the house and Crofs Street.

The actual use of this lateral addition is unknown. It is

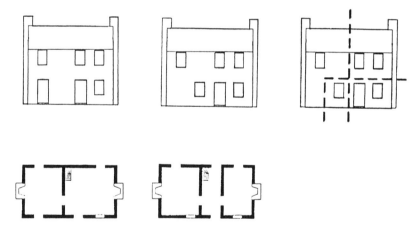

Figure 23. Evolution of fenestration and floorplans in the Robert Steele House, 1841–1856. The original hall-and-parlor floorplan and fenestration pictured at left was changed to accommodate the addition of a central passageway pictured at right. These changes had implications which went far beyond the mere reorganization of space, as they shaped patterns of domestic life, reflecting the larger cultural changes occurring throughout the Valley. The new fenestration came closer to meeting the Georgian ideal as shown by the dotted lines in the far right illustration. The fenestration to the right of the vertical dotted line evidenced the two-thirds Georgian design, whereas the fenestration below the horizontal dotted line evidenced a typical three-bay Georgian design for the first floor.

119

likely that the kitchen arrangement used by the Steeles' was continued. The addition contains a large room with a fireplace and separate front and rear doorways; a smaller room to the back was used for storage and as a pantry in later years. Interpreted in the context of other I-houses in Augusta County, the large room most likely served as a kitchen, as this was a common usage for such additions. The window and door moldings are decorative and the mantel exhibits fluted pilasters with unornamented end-blocks, frieze, and cornice, a style characteristic of the Greek Revival fashion (1830–1860).

The Steele House underwent multiple renovations only ten to twenty years after its construction. Not only had the prevailing patterns of domestic activity changed, but the large Beard family required more personal space. Several name changes occurred during these transition years: the "hall" became the "dining room," the "central passage" became the "hall," and the "parlor" retained its name awhile longer before becoming the "sitting or living room" by the turn of the nineteenth century.

The pervasiveness of the Georgian ideal is further evidenced in the evolution of older floorplans in some of Greenville's finer dwellings. Both the Smith Tavern and the Breckenridge-Vines House were modified to conform to the I-house ideal (cf. caption Figure 24). Just as the center hall floorplan shaped new domestic socialization patterns within the newer houses, so too did these patterns shape the evolution of floorplans in these older houses.

The Smith Tavern represents a more typical way of transforming a hall-and-parlor design into a central passageway configuration. Remember that the original house contained two rooms: the large heated hall and a smaller room located on the south end. A third room was added to the south end, and the room in the middle was turned into the central passageway by locating a doorway there. The original doorway to the hall was covered over. A large spiral staircase replaced the narrow single-run staircase, thus completing the transformation of the old parlor into an elegant entrance foyer. Since the lateral addition included two bays, the overall effect was

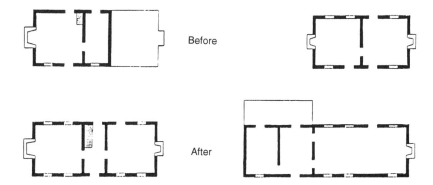

Figure 24. Evolution of fenestrations and floorplans in the Smith Tavern and Breckenridge-Vines House. The hall-and-parlor floorplans in the Smith Tavern and the Breckenridge-Vines House were changed to accommodate the addition of a central passageway. In the Smith Tavern (above left), the renovation involved building an addition onto the right side of the house, thereby allowing the parlor to be transformed into a central passageway. The doorway was moved to provide entrance into this passageway and allowed the windows to be arranged to produce a five-bay Georgian facade; clapboarding was added to unify the entire facade. In the Breckenridge-Vines House (above right), the renovation involved joining two separate hall-and-parlor houses by eliminating the common wall between them. The floorplan in the house on the right (the brick part) was transformed into a single room by removing the wall and staircase separating the hall from the parlor; the two front doorways were bricked over with one of them becoming a window. The fenestration in the left house (the frame part) was reversed so that the doorway opened into the central passageway thus completing the overall transformation. It is of note that the frame part originally had a central doorway flanked by two windows and had been modified once before, prior to the merging of the two houses. The magnetism of the central passage over the years is evident as the Smith Tavern renovations were completed around 1820; the Breckenridge-Vines House was altered in the 1940s — yet both owners strove for the same goals!

to enlarge the old three-bay facade to five bays. These renovations occurred between 1814 and 1840, about the same time that the brick ells were constructed to the rear of the house. An unusual renovation occurred more than 100 years later in 1953, attesting to the continuing desire to elevate the stature of the house: the log and frame portions were sheathed in a brick veneer to match the rear ells and give the entire structure a more unified appearance.

Figure 25. Altered fenestration of the Breckenridge-Vines House. The radical transformation of the four-bay hall-and-parlor house on the right (the brick part) and the three-bay hall-and-parlor house on the left to a central passageway floorplan can be seen in the unusual, "very stretched" fenestration of the Breckenridge-Vines House shown below. The north room is indeed spacious and resembles a ballroom!

Perhaps the most radical example of a hall-and-parlor floorplan reconfigured to produce a central passageway design is found in the Breckenridge-Vines House. In this case, two adjoining hall-and-parlor houses were combined! The board wall in the brick portion which divided the house into two equally-sized rooms was removed to produce a single (large) room on the north end. The parlor in the frame portion was transformed into a central passageway. The fenestration was changed to accommodate the new floorplan. The north doorway in the brick portion was bricked in and the adjoining doorway was replaced with a window; the four-bay window arrangement on the second floor was left unchanged. The door and window in the frame half were reversed so that the door opened into the central passageway; a larger staircase was built in this room transforming it into a greeting foyer just as it had been done in the Smith Tavern. These changes, dating to the 1940s, came late to the Breckenridge-Vines House.

16

Prosperity Continues

At this point, we shift our attention to the events surrounding the era of continued prosperity experienced by the Beard family in Greenville. As described earlier, many thousands of settlers streamed through town during the first half of the nineteenth century, as Greenville gained distinction as a major marketplace for southern Augusta County. Despite a slow start in the late 1790s, court records indicate that residency in Greenville more than doubled between 1820 and 1850. Many town lots were divided, as merchants vied for Main Street frontage.

In his *Gazetteer of Virginia*, Joseph Martin described the town in 1835 as including:

> *. . . an extensive manufacturing flour mill, a woolen manufactory, 3 general stores, 2 taverns, 1 academy, 2 tanyards, 2 saddlers, 2 tailors, 1 blacksmith shop, 1 cabinet maker, 1 wheelwright, 1 saddle-tree maker, 3 house carpenters, 1 hatter, and 4 boot and shoe makers.*

These businesses reflect the kinds of commerce that dominated the Greenville economy. Products from cattle were prominent; hides were tanned and fashioned into saddles, boots, and hats. Sheep farmers supplied raw materials to a woolen mill and two tailors were available to fashion clothing from the cloth produced. The "extensive" flour mill impressed Martin; its output must have been great, perhaps supporting a considerable trade. The blacksmith and wheelwright no doubt found much business among the many merchants and travelers passing through, the latter providing a healthy business for the tavern keepers. Finally, the rapidly growing town probably required all the carpenters and general stores it could muster.

Of particular interest is the hat industry in Greenville. Nellie Drexel noted in 1940 that a "hat manufacturing plant" was located on Back Street and specialized in "rabbit-fur and wool for the making of hats." Brake has suggested that the famous *Stetson* hat company had its roots in Greenville, although he readily notes that his findings are inconclusive. Brake has described this hat shop as being located in the basement of the Breckenridge-Vines House. As noted earlier, James Williamson and his wife Elizabeth operated a mantua and bonnet making business, but they did not own property in Greenville after 1822, and it is unclear whether their business was ever moved from Staunton to Greenville — an unlikely prospect.

Many Greenville merchants set up their shops in buildings that had been previously used as dwellings. The Breckenridge-Vines House, for example, has a long history of commercial use. Although the chronology is not clear, the building once housed a harness shop, a drug store, post office, and dentist office. Similarly, the Palmer House was the site of numerous general stores until the 1920s.

One business that brought renown to the Greenville area was the Bumgardner distillery located just west of town at Bethel Green (on Virginia Route 701). Beginning in the 1820s, M. J. Bumgardner produced a popular rye whiskey known throughout the upper Valley. Ironically, the distillery was located on a small stream directly across from Bethel Church. The "J. Bumgardner" brand became so popular that the business moved to Staunton in 1878 with the opening of a retail and wholesale store under the name *Bumgardner & McQuade*. In 1884, their product was described as follows in Townsend and Cornman's survey of Staunton institutions:

The specialty of the firm is the famous "J. Bumgardner," whiskey than which there is no brand in the market more popular and none more absolute pure in use. From Maine to Texas and from ocean to ocean, this brand of liquor has for half a century been the synonym of all that is desirable for medical purposes and for general use, and the Examining Commissioner of the Board of Health of New York city in 1869, declared this the only pure whiskey of the large number of samples sent them for examination.

As commerce grew rapidly, so also did the need for adequate roads in the Valley. Turnpike companies proliferated in the Valley between 1816 and 1860 to meet this demand. These turnpike companies agreed to improve existing roads and/or construct new additions in return for the right to charge fees to all users at tollgates along the way. The name "turnpike" referred to the "pike" or "pole" that stretched across the road. Only after the toll was paid was the pike lifted allowing the vehicle to pass.

Turnpikes became very popular by the mid-nineteenth century, resulting in the acceleration of road improvements throughout Augusta County between 1830 and 1860. Individual investors typically footed the bill with an eye towards receiving a handsome profit. The Staunton and James River Turnpike built in 1827 has already been described; however, in the years immediately following, several additional turnpike companies were formed which had a major impact upon Greenville's economy.

The Valley Turnpike Company was chartered around 1835 and improved ninety miles of the Great Road between Staunton and Winchester. The specifications called for a forty-foot wide roadway with the center eighteen-feet to consist of packed gravel (macadamized). Toll stations were placed every five miles. As might be expected, the Great Road became known as the Valley Pike by succeeding generations. Unfortunately for Greenville, the road going south of Staunton was not chartered as a turnpike until March, 1849. The road was to run from Staunton to Buchanan via Greenville. Instead of a macadamized roadway, the road was graded and constructed of wooden planks. It was during this period of construction that a roadway was built over Jack's Hill where US Route 11 is currently located and connected with the Main Street. Greenville now had three roads entering town from the north: the Staunton Road, the Ridge Road, and the Valley Pike.

Roads built of planks laid in a bed of gravel or placed upon half-buried timbers were becoming common in parts of rural America during the 1840s. The life of an oak road was considered to be about ten years, whereas a pine road would only last four years. Despite this limited lifespan, planks were preferred because they were not as hard on wagon wheels and horse hoofs as packed gravel. How long the plank road was maintained is not known; it probably did not last through the Civil War.

The first road connecting Greenville directly to markets east of the Blue Ridge was chartered in March 1848 with construction completed in the early 1850s. This road was called the Howardsville Turnpike and ran from Howardsville to the Rockfish River and then traversed the Blue Ridge at Howard's Gap. The turnpike then ran from Sherando to Stuarts Draft, where it turned south along parts of US Route 340 to Greenville. In March, 1856, the western section between Stuarts Draft and Greenville was renamed the Beverley Manor Turnpike. This turnpike was heavily used to ship livestock and produce to the James River at Howardsville, located several miles upstream from the port of Scottsville.

17

McCormick's Good Doctor

During this time of prosperity, the Robert Steele House changed hands a couple of times. Dr. Nimrod Hitt bought the house from the Beards for one-thousand dollars on May 28, 1856. He also owned most of King's Hill, the prominent knoll along the Great Road on the southwest border of town. Although he carried the title of doctor, there is no indication that he ever practiced medicine. In the 1850 census, Dr. Hitt is listed as a farmer living in Greenville with property valued at $2915 — quite well-to-do. He was fifty-two years old when he bought the house and was married to Elizabeth, aged forty-three.

In his forties, Dr. Hitt had achieved considerable notoriety as a witness during the public hearings held on March 17, 1848, at Steele's Tavern by the US Patent Office in which credit for inventing the *Virginia Reaper* was contested. Cyrus McCormick had originally received a patent for the reaper in 1834; however, his patent renewal was seriously challenged by another inventor named Obed Hussey who claimed to have developed a similar machine in 1833. Consequently, a hearing was set requiring McCormick to prove that the reaper was operational prior to that time. Dr. Hitt made a well-publicized, sworn statement to this effect on January 1, 1848, in which he detailed his having observed a demonstration of the reaper near Steele's Tavern in the Fall of 1831.

The essential part of Dr. Hitt's statement was as follows:

During the harvest of eighteen hundred and thirty-one, whilst boarding at the house of Mr. Jno. Steele, about one mile from the farm of Mr. Robt. McCormick, decd., father of Cyrus H., I had notice that a machine had been constructed by the latter to cut wheat (or other small grain) and that a trial of it could be seen on said farm on that day. I, accordingly, as well as Mr. and Mrs. Steele, went to Mr. McCormicks and did on that day witness probably one of the first experiments made of the "Virginia Reaper."

Upon direct questioning, Hitt also reported having witnessed the "construction" of the reaper by both Robert and Cyrus McCormick. Although the patent was not renewed, this testimony was instrumental in supporting Cyrus' claim as the inventor of the reaper. There has been some speculation regarding how well Dr. Hitt had been prepared and compensated by the McCormicks for his valuable testimony.

The McCormick farm, named "Walnut Grove," is located about a mile west of Steele's Tavern and eight miles from Greenville. By the late 1840s, the "Reaper" was widely marketed for around fifty dollars although sales were initially low. The machine required two horses and two men to operate it; its makers claimed it could cut about two acres of wheat per hour. Cyrus McCormick moved production of the Reaper to Chicago in 1847 where the McCormick Harvesting Machine Company flourished, marketing the Reaper worldwide. This company evolved into the International Harvester Corporation which dominated the farm equipment industry well into the twentieth century. One can only wonder if Dr. Hitt appreciated the significance of what he and a few others had witnessed during that fateful day in the fall of 1831.

Dr. Hitt lived in the house only a short time, as he sold the 10 acres of land comprising Kings Hill adjoining the "plank road" and the house and lot in Greenville "on which the said Hitt resides" for $1500 on January 19, 1857. He apparently moved to the Lofton area where he died in 1863. He left a respectable estate, including other land holdings and slaves, to his wife and young daughter, Calladonia. Unfortunately, his daughter died shortly thereafter on the day before Christmas, 1865, at age seven.

The new owners of the house were listed on the deed as Bumgardner and McClure. Andrew W. McClure, a young man of thirty-one years, was married to Mary Bumgardner, daughter of Lewis and Holly Ann. The young couple bought the house and land with her parents. It is not known whether one or both couples lived in the house. Both Lewis Bumgardner and Andrew McClure were merchants in Greenville and perhaps worked together. It is likely that their business was of the "general store or dry goods" variety since neither was described as having a specific trade in the US Census or court records. After two years, the business was moved to Staunton and the family sold the house and town lot, minus the 10 acres, on January 8, 1859. Dr. John Tate bought the house for two dollars plus mortgage and it was during this time that part of the house might have served as an office for medical practice.

Not much is known about Dr. Tate, although he was a member of Greenville's esteemed Tate family. We can speculate about how it was to be a medical practitioner in Greenville before the Civil War. Country doctoring epitomized the phrase, "American ingenuity," as rural life was filled with many perils. Infectious diseases such as smallpox, typhoid, and diphtheria ravaged the countryside where sanitation practices were poor and the risks of bacterial infection and contagion were virtually unknown. Farm and milling accidents were particularly alarming due to the deadly threat of infection.

Dr. Tate very likely worked from sunrise to twilight, traveling over rough terrain to make home visits in the early morning and evening; office hours in town were typically held in the afternoon. It was a demanding occupation that did not pay much. His treatments included a combination of folk remedies and standard medical treatments such as amputation and bloodletting which themselves were often as life-threatening as the ailment itself. Despite their outward respect for the medical profession and Dr. Tate, most Greenville residents probably relied upon their own home remedies, especially alcohol for pain, before risking a call for the Doctor.

18

Greenville in the Civil War

As differences between the northern and southern states regarding the issues of states' rights, slavery, and equal representation in Congress intensified throughout 1859 and 1860, the people of Augusta rallied for the Union. To this end, on November 26, 1860, a committee met in the Augusta County courthouse to prepare a formal statement on the issue of secession. Their views were eloquently stated by Hugh W. Sheffey, quoted in part as follows:

> ... that our senators and delegates be requested to bend their energies to keep Virginia to her moorings as 'flag ship of the union,' and to induce her, placed as she is between the north and the extreme south, with moderation, forbearance and wisdom worthy of her ancient renown, to exert her power and influence to preserve, on the one hand, the known and equal rights of her own people as citizens of a common country, and, on the other hand, the harmony of the union and the integrity of the constitution.

Unfortunately, this position did not hold. Following the surrender of Fort Sumter in April, 1861, and President Abraham Lincoln's proclamation calling for seventy thousand volunteer soldiers, the Virginia Convention passed an ordinance of secession. Augusta County was left without any option, feeling that they had been forced into the conflict through a federal violation of state's rights.

Soon thereafter, numerous companies of militia were organized throughout the County. In Greenville, Captain James W. Newton organized a company of local men who named themselves the "Augusta Greys." Other companies organized about the same time were the "Southern Guard" from Middlebrook and the "Valley Rangers" from Waynesboro.

On April 17, 1861, all business in Staunton was suspended as these companies gathered from throughout the County. It was an exciting time: crowds turned out to cheer the soldiers. Speeches were given; goodbyes were exchanged. For the next two days, company after company left Staunton and marched northward along the Valley Turnpike to occupy the federal armory located at Harpers Ferry.

Upon arrival at the armory, the companies from Augusta County were organized into the Fifth Virginia Regiment, commanded by Colonel Thomas J. Jackson. This unit later became known as the "Stonewall Brigade" following the first battle at Manassas in July, 1861. Here Jackson and the regiment were made famous by holding their position, like a stone wall, during a concentrated Union onslaught which came at a particularly strategic point in the battle.

Although no descriptions of daily life in Greenville during the early part of the war exist, much can be gleaned from the accounts of observers in Staunton. Since Staunton served as a major supply depot for the southern armies in both eastern and western Virginia, all roads in Augusta County were busy with supply wagons and incoming troops from the Deep South. Since Greenville was situated on one of the two major routes between Lexington and Staunton, much of the activity in Greenville can be inferred from descriptions of arrivals and departures in Staunton.

In April of that first year, many guns and cannons were transported to Staunton from Lexington. Long trains with sixty or more wagons passed through Greenville throughout the summer of 1861. Endless columns of troops, some from as far away as Georgia, marched through town, sending up clouds of dust which could be seen for miles. In addition, purchasing agents from Staunton frequently came into town soliciting from area farmers: produce, livestock, horses, and wagons. Women from all over Augusta County were commissioned to provide army uniforms, produce flags, and prepare foodstuffs. The urgency of providing supplies to the southern troops was revealed in the May 19, 1861, diary entry of Dr. McFarland, the minister of Bethel Church:

Young Mr. Trout came with nearly 300 yards of plaid linsey to make shirts for the soldiers, with a note that they wanted 1000 made by Tuesday night — They were sending the work round to the different cong'ns. Our ladies appointed to meet at the ch. tomorrow morning.

By the middle of the summer, the horrors of war were close at hand, as engagements with the Union forces were occurring less than seventy miles to the west in towns like Philippi where the Southern armies suffered an early defeat. The wounded were brought back to Staunton and surrounding towns. These initial glimpses of wartime suffering were clearly described by a diarist in Staunton on July 20, 1861, and quoted by Waddell:

On Thursday evening two wagons full of sick soldiers arrived from Monterey, Highland County. Before these could be provided for, others were brought in . . . the sight was a sickening one — one man gasping with asthma, another burning with fever, and another shaking with chills. There are now at least one hundred and fifty sick soldiers in town. The citizens are doing what they can for them.

Staunton and many surrounding towns were overrun with sick and wounded soldiers. Meanwhile, new companies of soldiers continued to be formed from the available men and boys throughout the county.

As the war continued, resources became scarce and prices for necessities rose dramatically. Small towns like Greenville suffered heavily, losing not only access to goods from larger cities like Staunton, where most goods were earmarked for the military, but also losing its own resources in the form of wagons, horses, and men impressed for military service. All coins disappeared and small town economies were forced to rely on bartering.

Reports on the progress of the war were anxiously awaited by all, though they were often delayed, conflicting, and erroneous. It was not long before the threat of invasion caused a panic in the Augusta citizenry. In mid-April of 1862, a Union force of about four-thousand troops advanced from the west as far as McDowell, with some troops reported to be as close as Buffalo Gap, just ten miles outside Staunton. This invasion was halted by the maneuvers of General Thomas J. Jackson and his Stonewall Brigade. The Union Army was defeated first at McDowell, then at Front Royal, Winchester, Cross Keys, and Port Republic.

In a three-month span, the small southern army of about fifteen-thousand men marched over six-hundred miles, fought, and defeated three Union armies totaling over sixty-thousand troops. This feat was a continuing source of pride for the Greenville men who participated, for to have served with Jackson was to be immortalized in the pages of Valley history. Following this campaign the threat of invasion was gone, although the faint rumblings of cannon could be heard in the Valley from the direction of Richmond.

As the war dragged into the summer of 1864, the Union armies pressed towards the upper Valley in hopes of stopping the steady flow of produce and livestock supplying the Southern Army east of the Blue Ridge. The imminent threat of invasion again stirred anxieties throughout Augusta County, much as it had in 1862. It was feared that the Union forces would destroy what few resources remained in the Valley. Consequently, frantic attempts were made to enlist any man, young or old, able to fire a rifle.

Despite suffering an embarrassing defeat outside the town of New Market in early May, the Union Army quickly reorganized under General David Hunter and advanced south into Augusta County. General Hunter had earned a reputation as a vindictive man, bent on punishing the South by burning buildings and looking away as his troops plundered civilian property. He was called "Black Dave." News that he was advancing up the Valley must have been horrific. To make matters worse, a second Union Army under Generals George Crook and William Averill was on the march from the west, heading for Buffalo Gap. The Southern Army, largely made up of inexperienced young boys, old men, and Valley farmers, chose to meet General Hunter's force first. Under the command of General William Jones, the Confederate Army engaged the Bluecoats just north of New Hope.

As Waddell aptly wrote, "no resident of Staunton then living and over the age of infancy will ever forget Sunday, June 5, 1864." Soon after daybreak, an anxious populace crowded on the hilltops surrounding Staunton, watching as an ominous smoke rose along the northern horizon. No news was available for most of the day, engendering a mounting feeling of uneasiness. It was not until late afternoon that the distinctive din of cannon added to the spectacle, signaling that a pitched battle was underway. Under the direction of Colonel Edwin G. Lee, Staunton's commandant, all foodstuffs, ammunition, and government records were hastily loaded onto wagons and freight cars, and the trains made ready for evacuation. The news arrived just before sunset: General Jones had been killed and his army was routed.

A letter dated June 6th by James Short aptly described the defeat in no uncertain terms:

> . . . we had to run so hard that we was give out when we got thare I never seen the like of the balls in all of my life . . . we fot right hard for some time and we had to run like thunder . . . the yankees would have got all of them if they had not run.

Back in Staunton, Colonel Lee immediately directed the wagon train and freight cars to leave town while a second train was loaded up to follow. The wagons stopped near Greenville for the night, leaving early next morning to cross the Blue Ridge at Tye River Gap. Many frightened citizens, personal belongings in hand, crowded behind the wagons, leaving their homes to the invaders.

It was the arrival of this wagon train that brought the terrible news to Greenville. Like their neighbors in Staunton, they had probably watched the smoke rise from the north and anxiously awaited news about the battle. Undoubtedly, several Greenville citizens joined the groups hurrying south along the Valley Turnpike to escape General Hunter's Army.

As expected, the Union Army swarmed into Staunton the next day and remained there most of the week. During this period, much of the town was ransacked; all depots, railroad facilities, and mills were destroyed. On the morning of June tenth, the Union Army divided into three columns — all headed south towards Lexington. One column traveled along the Middlebrook-Brownsburg Turnpike; another column marched towards Waynesboro, turning south along the base of the Blue Ridge. The main column, including both infantry and artillery, advanced towards Greenville. General Hunter traveled with this last column, arriving in Greenville around noon.

Although few written descriptions of General Hunter's march through Greenville exist, it is easy to imagine the fear invoked as the Union troops surged down Main Street. News of burnings and lootings in Staunton had been arriving all the previous week; these fears were justified. Upon arriving in Greenville, the army reduced two mills to heaps of smoldering ashes. The first mill, known as "Smith's" or "Acorn Mill," was located on the South River at the southwest corner of town. The stone mill dam was the same one owned by James Mitchell in 1819. Greenville lore has it that the army was unable to destroy the dam despite several attempts. This dam still exists, although it was covered with cement in the early 1900s. The site of the second mill is not documented but it might have been located two miles northwest of Greenville where the stone mill runs can be seen along Virginia Route 701.

Aside from military records, two oral accounts of Greenville's occupation have been passed down. The first is a conversation recorded by John Brake in 1948 with an elderly black man named George McKany who once worked as a custodian at the Greenville High School. McKany reported that he watched Yankee soldiers burn the old mill when he was about thirteen years-old in 1864.

The second anecdote comes from an historical sketch of the Greenville Methodist Church prepared by Reverend Harry W. Craver in 1936. In this sketch he reported that Rev. Mr. Lambeth was seated on the porch of the Graham home in Greenville when Hunter's brigade passed by, taking and destroying property. Rev. Mr. Lambeth displayed a Masonic emblem and the Graham home was spared from plunder and destruction. That respect for the Masonic emblem took precedence over the spoils of war perhaps underscores the sense of ambivalence that the Union soldiers must have felt as they invaded the communities of their former countrymen. The Graham House still stands today on the corner of Main and Crofs streets, cater-cornered to the Steele House, on lot 9. This latter anecdote is revealing in another way as it suggests that most homes in Greenville were plundered. It is likely that the Steele House was among them, as it was made of brick and was stately in appearance. It certainly would have been ransacked if it were known to be the home of two Confederate soldiers.

General Hunter's columns did not stay in Greenville long, but continued on, camping near Steele's Tavern before advancing through Fairfield and arriving at Lexington the next day. Numerous wagons lagged behind carrying supplies and wounded Union soldiers. This was perhaps Greenville's darkest hour, following three hard years of scraping together men and supplies for the war effort.

Several Greenville area residents distinguished themselves during the war. Of highest repute were the Doak and Lilley brothers. General Robert Doak Lilley received his commission as a Major in Company D of the Twenty-fifth Virginia Infantry. He was promoted to Brigadier General in May, 1864, and commanded a brigade in the third battle of Winchester where his right arm was shattered near the shoulder by a minié ball. He commanded the Valley reserves until the end of the war. General Lilley served as a delegate to the Synod of Virginia after the war and died an early death, in 1886, from complications from his wounds.

His younger brother, Colonel John Doak Lilley, left his studies at the Virginia Military Institute in Lexington and joined Company H of the Fifty-second Virginia Infantry as a First Lieutenant. He participated in several major engagements and was severely wounded in the left thigh in the second battle of Manassas in August, 1862. After convalescing, he rejoined the field in 1864 but again was seriously wounded while leading a charge near Spottsylvania. Promoted to Lieutenant Colonel in May, 1864, John Lilley fought with General Jubal Early in the battle of Waynesboro in March, 1865. Despite having suffered many wounds, John Lilley attained the rank of Colonel in the Virginia militia after the war and worked as a surveyor and school board member until his death in June, 1913.

The youngest brother, James Campbell Lilley, left his employment as a surveyor and enlisted as a Fourth Sergeant in Company I of the Fifty-second Virginia Infantry. He was seventeen years old. Initially, he served as a courier to General Thomas J. Jackson, but later became a sharpshooter. James Lilley fought on many battlefields without receiving wounds. After the war, he studied engineering under the tutelage of the esteemed Jed Hotchkiss at Washington University. After a serving as Staunton City Engineer, he left Virginia to work in Mexico for the Mexican Central Railroad where he passed away in 1901.

19

A Family Endures

Dr. Tate sold the house on June 11, 1863, only three weeks before the battle of Gettysburg and the fall of Vicksburg. The new owner was Sarah McGilvray, a widowed mother of eleven children, who paid six dollars plus mortgage for the property.

Sarah McGilvray had relatives in Greenville; she was born in May, 1803, to Jacob Bumgardner and his wife and married Colonel Alexander McGilvray at nearby Bethel Church in 1820. Her husband was a gunsmith who died in 1853 at age fifty-five while the family lived in Harrisonburg. Sarah McGilvray returned to Greenville after his passing. She was sixty years-old when she bought the house, moving in with her six children: Lewis Tazewell (aged thirty), Harriet (aged twenty-eight), Martha (aged twenty-six), Hester (aged twenty-three), Sarah (aged twenty), and Althealeane (aged sixteen).

Once again the house was home to a large family. Her son, Lewis T. McGilvray, worked as a "skilled artisan" and "gunsmith", having learned his trade from his father. He fashioned decorative long arms and provided support for his widowed mother and five sisters.

The Civil War took its toll on the McGilvray family. Alexander McGilvray, a relative who formerly worked as a tailor in Greenville, was one of the original members of the Confederate militia organized by Captain James W. Newton in Greenville. This unit marched out on April 19, 1861, to become part of the Stonewall Brigade. Alexander McGilvray served early in the war at Harpers Ferry and First Manassas as the company drummer before becoming wounded and receiving a medical discharge in November, 1861. In addition, in 1862, Lewis T. McGilvray joined the "Valley Guards" which became Company G of the Tenth Virginia Infantry, also serving under General Thomas J. Jackson. Lewis received wounds and was subsequently discharged; he returned to Greenville.

The passing of Sarah McGilvray in March, 1865, coincided with the end of the Civil War which was followed by a period of intense economic depression throughout the southern states. The poor post-war economy was reflected in the settlement of the McGilvray estate which was heavily in debt to local merchants. At the time of her death, her debt totaled $2,012.83.

Although foodstuffs were scarce in Greenville during the war, they were not unobtainable. The town's distance from the grip of Staunton's commissary officers coupled with support from local farmers helped insulate Greenville from the extreme shortages of goods routinely suffered by larger cities. Prices did rise, but primarily for imported goods like salt, sugar, and coffee.

The most frequently purchased items noted in McGilvray's ledger included pork, beef, flour, corn meal, butter, and sugar; produce was grown at home. Greenville prices during the war were listed as follows:

> . . . 45 lb of bacon, $5.62; 27 lbs of ham, $2.47; four chickens, $0.50; two dozen herring, $0.50; one barrel flour, $5.00; one bushel meal, $0.55; one barrel cider, $2.00; 1½ lbs coffee, $0.25; two dozen eggs, $0.25; 2½ bushels apples, $1.25.

The estate settlement provides a rare glimpse of a household inventory which was sold at public auction in July, 1866, for a total of $112.17. The inventory reveals the modesty of the estate. Among the most valuable possessions were twelve silver spoons valued at $12.50 and a feather bed with two pillows valued at fifteen dollars. Few items of comfort were mentioned: only two pairs of window curtains and three floor coverings were listed. Since the estate sale was supervised by the court, coupled with the observation that family members, particularly Lewis McGilvray, were among the auction bidders, it appears that the estate listing was complete.

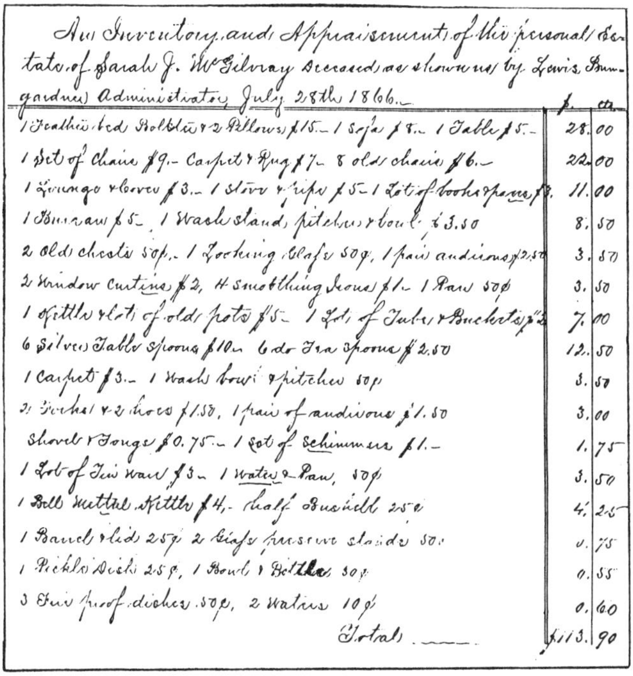

An Inventory and Appraisement of the personal Estate of Sarah J. McGilvray deceased as shown us by Lewis Baumgardner Administrator July 28th 1866.—

	$	cts
1 Feather bed Bolster & 2 Pillows $15.— 1 Sofa $8.— 1 Table $5.—	28.	00
1 Set of Chairs $9.— Carpet & Rug $7— 8 old chairs $6.—	22.	00
1 Lounge & Cover $3.— 1 Stove & pipe $5— 1 Lot of books & papers $3.	11.	00
1 Bureau $5— 1 Wash stand, pitcher & bowl $3.50	8.	50
2 old chests 50¢.— 1 Looking Glass 50¢, 1 pair andirons $2.50	3.	50
2 Window Curtains $2, 4 smoothing Irons $1— 1 Pan 50¢	3.	50
1 Kettle & lot of old pots $5— 1 Lot of Tubs & Buckets $2	7.	00
6 Silver Table spoons $10— 6 do Tea spoons $2.50	12.	50
1 Carpet $3.— 1 Wash bowl & pitcher 50¢	3.	50
2 Forks & 2 hoes $1.50, 1 pair of andirons $1.50	3.	00
Shovel & Tongs $0.75— 1 Lot of Skimmers $1.—	1.	75
1 Lot of Tin ware $3— 1 Water Pan, 50¢	3.	50
1 Bell mettal Kettle $4,— half Bushel 25¢	4.	25
1 Barrel & lid 25¢ 2 Glass preserve stands 50¢	0.	75
1 Pickle Dish 25¢, 1 Bowl & Bottles 30¢	0.	55
3 Fire proof dishes 50¢, 2 Waiters 10¢	0.	60
Total ———	$113.	90

Figure 26. Estate inventory of Sarah McGilvray, 1866.

Sarah McGilvray's estate inventory prompts a closer look at home life in Greenville during the 1860s and the decades just preceding the war. It is easy to forget that the McGilvrays, Tates, McClures, Hitts, Beards, and even Robert Steele all lived in an unlit, unheated, uninsulated brick house without toilets, baths, or running water. As the McGilvray inventory reveals, heat was provided by a "stove and pipe" and two pairs of "andirons" for the fireplaces. The kitchen with its cookstove was located in the lateral addition; old burns char the mantel located there. The remaining three hearths in the parlor, dining room, and south bedroom provided heat in the winter.

It would become so cold and drafty in early January and February that the family would huddle close to the fire, nearly scorching themselves, to keep warm. The far corners of the house would drop below freezing at night, particularly when the fire burned low. Heating was not efficient, and multiple cords of wood were consumed during the cold season. It was a dirty time with wood chips and ash tracked all through the house.

Water was carried in from a cistern located near the north side of the yard. McGilvray's estate included two "wash pitchers and bowls", a tub and several buckets or "waters." Bathing was a luxury. Typically, a family would share a single tub of water: children first, mothers and daughters next, and then the men — the bath was dark and murky when it was finally dumped off the back porch. It was hard work hefting buckets of water into the house, and so very little was wasted, particularly during the summer droughts.

The McGilvray dining room was sparsely appointed with wooden chairs and table; the parlor had a carpet, a sofa, and a "lounge and cover." Curtains adorned the windows in the two best rooms. Other furniture included "old chests" and a "feather bed." The latter referred to a straw-filled mattress supported by ropes threaded upon a simple frame or "bed-stead" giving rise to night time sayings such as "sleep tight" (tight ropes were important for support and comfort) and "don't let the bed bugs bite" (there were often six and eight legged critters living in the straw).

Lighting presented a number of problems. Candle-making was costly and labor-intensive. That most nineteenth century families dipped their own candles is a myth. A glob of animal fat with a wick sufficed for many well past the antebellum days. It was not uncommon for a household to possess only one candle holder or sconce. Well-to-do households were often characterized by the number of candles burned at night; for example, a "three-candle family" was very wealthy. But for the common folk, it is generally believed that most chores and reading were completed before dark, and that bedtime

144

came with the setting sun. Sometimes the head of household, usually the father or patriarch, would keep a candle stick hooked on the back of a favorite chair; this is why so many old ladderbacks show telltale burn marks along the top slat.

Odd as it may seem, domestic life during the middle half of the nineteenth century was not as lavish on the inside as the fine Georgian facades would proclaim on the outside. Of course, the "very wealthy" enjoyed detached kitchens, servants, and many candles — allowing the formalized room arrangement of the center hall I-house to be exploited to its full advantage. The parlor and dining rooms were for leisure and not to be cluttered with the trappings of domestic chores. As such, a detached kitchen, lateral wing, or rear ell was essential to the I-house design, for the main house was more formal than practical in its arrangement. For most folks, like the McGilvrays, domestic life was more mundane, even tedious; day-to-day activities were characterized chiefly by household chores, hardships, and problems to be solved — put that way, not much has changed for most of us.

20

Prosperity Renewed

Our postwar history begins when Lewis T. McGilvray purchased his family home seventeen years after his mother's passing. Although much of Augusta County recovered soon after the war due to its bountiful agricultural resources, many families struggled long and hard to rebuild their lives after the war. McGilvray bought the house at public auction on May 31, 1882, for $1153. It is unknown whether the house was inhabited during the 1870s; however, it is likely that some of the McGilvray family lived there until the estate was settled. The deed of sale outlined a series of payments to be made to Sarah McGilvray's heirs.

In the 1880s, McGilvray established residence in the house, but he devoted much of his time to living at and developing a nearby mountain resort to the east called "Cold Spring." Apparently, he was absent from town enough for the August 18, 1882, issue of the *Greenville Banner* to report on his whereabouts:

Mr. McGilvray sent us a message to the effect that he had not hied himself away out there alone, as we intimated several weeks ago, but that he had with him a company of about sixty-five persons, torch-light danc-ing, music, & c., at the Cold Spring, upon the grounds of which camp he has labored season after season, until now it is a very attractive and pleasant place to put in the summer.

Barely a month later, this paper again reported:

. . . it is proposed to change the name of that popular mountain summer resort near here from Cold Spring to McGilvray Park, in honor of

Mr. L. Tazewell McGilvray, to whose indefatigable zeal and exertions the place is what it is, and to whom the people who go there in warm weather to find a delightful retreat are indebted for the same . . .

Even the *Staunton Vindicator* picked-up the story on August 17, 1883, publishing a more personal description of McGilvray and his resort, referring to him affectionately as Tazzy.

. . . an old bachelor, of no matrimonial pretentions, went to a place known as "cold spring" in the blue ridge and camped in tents, and annually since has returned and spent the summer alone, save a visit occasionally from some male acquaintance. This summer quite a number of citizens, who had formerly visited this place, determined to break the monotony of Tazzy, and therefore have erected five cabins on the grounds and are there with their families enjoying the pure air of the hitherto isolated place . . .

Certainly, Lewis McGilvray drew attention to himself. An old photo shows him to be a tall and slender man with a long, eccentric beard extending well down his chest. He was industrious, yet appeared to have shied away from publicity — hence, he engendered much curiosity in Greenville. When he passed away in 1902, his obituary described Tazwell as "a mechanician of exceptional ability and before the war, made a rifle for a man going to California that was inlaid with gold and silver. It was finally sold for a large sum and is now in a museum in San Francisco."

In his will dated June, 1900, he stipulated that the house be made available to whomever in the family might need a place to live; however, it is unknown whether his offer was taken, as the house passed from the McGilvray family to Roy and Olivia Hanger in 1902 for six-hundred dollars.

The house was unaltered except for the addition of a full-length Victorian porch, decorated with elaborate Eastlake trim. This porch appears in photographs taken as early as the late 1880s, suggesting that McGilvray had made some improvements to the house shortly after purchasing it. It was during this time that the window sash was updated to hold larger glass (two window panes per sash versus the original six panes per sash). The rear windows were left unchanged, as they could not be seen from the street.

McGilvray's initial development of Cold Spring paralleled economic resurgence in Greenville. A major contributing factor was the railroad. Staunton had enjoyed rail service since the mid-1850s; at the outbreak of the Civil War, the Virginia Central Railroad ran as far west as Clifton Forge, Virginia. Despite near total destruction at the hands of Union troops, the expansion of the railroads after the war was furious. In 1870, the Shenandoah Valley Railroad Company (SVRR) was organized to build a north-south route via Waynesboro to Roanoke City. The rails for this route were laid one mile to the east of Greenville along Poor Creek; the sounds of the first steam locomotive enroute to Roanoke City were heard in June, 1882.

Following Crofs Street west from Greenville, a loading ramp was located alongside the tracks. The railroad was warmly welcomed, and before long a small station, post office, and several stores sprung up along the edges of the creek basin. The post office was called Ellard. This depot was located where Virginia Route 662 crosses the creek. The line is presently operated by the Norfolk Southern Corporation and continues regular freight service today.

In 1878, the Baltimore and Ohio (B&O) Railroad endeavored to extend the old Valley Railroad from Staunton to Lexington; the Valley Railroad had nearly gone bankrupt trying to complete this line several years earlier. Many of the difficulties encountered involved building bridges across the many creekbeds. The rocky bluffs and steep ravine along the South River presented a particular problem. Financing was approved by the County Board of Supervisors for a concrete bridge but was later rescinded when it was found out how much it would cost! A wooden trestle was built. With such delays, progress was slow; the editorials of the day underscored Greenville's impatience. The last sections were finally laid in the fall of 1883, bringing the B&O line to a station located on the west border of Greenville.

The old railroad bed is visible from US Route 11 to the west as you approach Greenville from Staunton. The station is

Figure 27. B&O Railroad station in Greenville, circa 1883. Located along the west border of town, the Greenville railroad station connected merchants with the ever-expanding national economy. Almost immediately, the area along the railroad tracks proliferated with warehouses and stockyards to capitalize upon the shipping opportunities brought by the freight trains which passed daily.

no longer standing, but the earthen supports for the trestle which once spanned the South River are still visible. The most enduring evidence of the rail line are the many buildings that were built on the hill just west of town. This area grew quickly and became the site of large stock yards, produce-packing plants and hotels.

A series of surveys, dating February, 1889, and July, 1911, detailed the laying of town lots on the west side of town, behind Back Street. This area was called the "Palmer Addition," and as development progressed, was dubbed "New Greenville." The land bordering the railroad was prudently divided into ten lots to promote commercial development along the tracks; thirty-two additional lots were surveyed for residential use. Although the construction of houses lagged behind business development, this trend was reversed by 1920, as many large dwellings were built here. A third annexation, dated May, 1903, and known as the "McDonald Addition," was surveyed in the interim along the west side of the Valley Pike just north of the South River. All told, Greenville had more than doubled in size.

The dawning of the railroad era deserves further attention, for it dramatically altered the character of rural marketplaces like Greenville. Coupled with rapid industrialization in the northern cities, many new mass-produced products became available to rural residents via the railroad. In addition, advances in the preservation and packaging of foods allowed for canned produce, meats, and fish to be easily transported. As a result, Greenville merchants could stock their shelves with a wider variety of nationally-marketed brands than ever before.

These changes had a lasting impact upon how day-to-day business transactions were conducted in Greenville. For the first time, the stores in Greenville began to appear more similar to their city counterparts. National merchandisers provided stores with colorful signage and product dispensers. Fixed prices for mass-produced items became the norm, as antebellum bartering customs became obsolete. Following the precedent set by the emerging "giant stores" like F. W. Woolworth (established in 1879) and Kroger (established in 1885), rural stores began to stock "five and dime" merchandise. In addition, prepackaged goods replaced bulk purchases; for example, chewing tobacco could be purchased in individual bags instead of ten-pound loaves and coffee was available by the pound in tin containers rather than in scoops from the barrel.

Despite these changes, many traditions persisted. The stores in Greenville continued to operate on a non-cash basis well into the 1920s, with the practice continuing even longer for well-known residents. In contrast, cash and carry merchandising dominated urban stores by 1890. Greenville residents typically maintained an account ledger of purchases bought on credit to be paid in weekly or monthly intervals.

The 1893 ledger of John A. Frenger reveals some prices paid for items purchased from John H. Clarke, proprietor of a

"General Merchandise" store located in the Masons' Building on Greenville's Main Street. This ledger includes frequently purchased essentials such as sugar (five pounds at thirty-five cents), coffee (one pound at twenty-eight cents) and tobacco (one package at ten cents). In contrast, specialty items such as sarsaparilla (one bottle at ninety cents) were more expensive. The mention of items by trade name became common, for example a package of "Bob Diggs" for fifty cents and a package of "M. Meads" for nineteen cents.

A newspaper entitled the *Greenville Banner* was established by J. B. Burwell in June, 1882, and continued to circulate until early 1885. Subtitled "Everybody's friend — Nobody's enemy," this four-page weekly catered to local area news and gossip. During its brief publication, the *Banner* provided a rare glimpse of Greenville economics during the early 1880s. Several quotations from this paper paint a picture of a growing town aspiring to become a major marketplace, yet struggling to compete with the larger cities of Staunton and Waynesboro.

In describing the Depot at Ellard, the *Banner* reported in September, 1882:

> *The institution is one of great convenience and supplies a want long felt by our people who have produce to ship and goods of various kinds to import from other points, as it saves much labor and time in hauling to and from Staunton, formerly the nearest railroad station, affording as it does ample accommodation for passengers, baggage, handling and storage of freight, shipping produce, stock, & etc. Considerable business is there transacted daily, and in addition to conveniences already named we have between town and the depot a double daily mail, no small item for business men.*

Cattle were driven through Greenville on a near-daily basis and wagon loads of produce crowded Main Street. Rival market towns such as Middlebrook and Brownsburg were unable to compete, having been completely bypassed by the railroads. The competition with Staunton merchants was evident in Burwell's comment "that our farmers are hauling their flour to Greenville depot, leaving Staunton out in the cold." Furthermore, Burwell boasted, " . . . in this place you

Figure 28. Palmer storehouse in 1890 (top). This storehouse opened after the Civil War and operated until the building was renovated in the late 1930s (bottom). The left half of the building contains a two-story log house built soon after the town was founded.

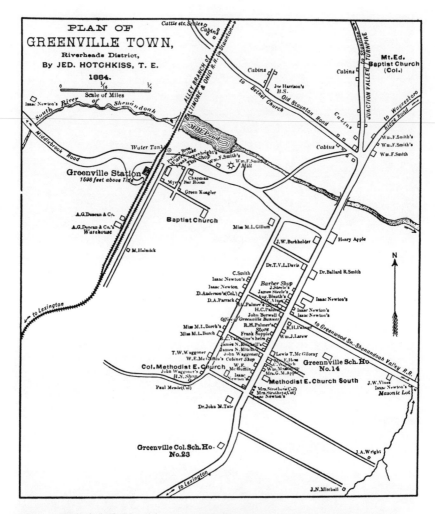

Figure 29. Jedidiah Hotchkiss map of Greenville, 1884. The map depicts Greenville during prosperous times. The B&O Railroad had just arrived a year earlier, and the town was poised to grow once again, as it had in the 1820s, into a thriving marketplace. The beginnings of New Greenville can be seen along the B&O tracks. Over ninety buildings are shown on the map with thirty-five of them located along Main Street.

can now get almost any article you call for, and at a reasonable cost. A much better variety of goods have a place in our stores now than ever known before in this town's history."

A letter to the Editor from Moffatt's Creek in the September 29, 1882, edition of the *Banner*, spoke highly of Greenville.

I have not been in Greenville for nearly two years, and was pleased to see the improvements which had taken place in the village during that time, notably those of messrs. H.C. and R.H. Palmer, both of whom have enlarged and greatly improved their storehouses, and the latter erected a very neat, comfortable dwelling. The Palmer brothers are go-ahead fellows, whose energy in business is only equaled by their genial hospitality. All success to the whole-souled Palmer boys. The Greenville hotel, having been remodeled and renovated, will, I hope, under the management of its present courteous and accommodating proprietor, J. Ballard Smith, receive a liberal share of patronage, which I feel assured it merits. Greenville, for its size, is well supplied with bar-rooms, having two of those establishments, both located in the business center of the town, and doubtless well supplied with all the necessary appliances for refreshing inner man, each contiguous to the other, so that the thirsty Greenvillians, as well as transient visitors, may fire and fall back "ad libitum."

Of interest, the Palmer stores marketed a cigar aptly named "Greenville Sports."

In November, 1882, Burwell listed all the Greenville merchants then in business, enumerated as follows:

1. H. C. Palmer
2. A. G. Duncan — "New York Cash Store"
3. Palmer & Hammond — successors to R. H. Palmer
4. Mrs. Jennie L. Palmer — Millinery store
5. Mrs. Mitchell, Ms. Burch, Ms. Lohr, Mrs. Hess — Mantua
6. James Steele, W. J. Larew — Saloons
7. Henry Apple, D. A. Parrick & son — Boot and shoe shop
8. Prof. J. A. Wright — Musical instrument agency
9. Jewett Vines esg. — Saddlery
10. J. W. Vines — Confectionery & Saddlery
11. J. N. Mitchell — Tailoring house
12. Wm. F. Smith, Wm. Apple — Tanneries
13. Dr. Tate — "Medicine man"
14. Wm. McGiffin — "Furniture man"
15. Fitch & Keiser — Painters
16. J. Almarod esq. — Sewing machine agent
17. Robert Selby, J. M. Lohr — Carpenters
18. R. C. Valentine — Jeweler
19. Wagner, Jos. Harrison — Blacksmith shops
20. Greenville mills
21. Greenville hotel

For services not immediately available in town, Greenville residents relied upon traveling salesmen, photographers, dentists, and the like. The *Banner* would advertise these services with notices such as, "Dr. W. A. Jones, the dentist, will be in the Greenville Hotel for two or three days." Greenville did eventually get its own dentist, Dr. Shultz, who established his office in the south corner room of the Breckenridge-Vines House in the 1930s.

One of the first large employers of Greenville residents was the Cold Spring Mining Company established near the turn of the century. The chalk mines were located just east of town along the west face of the Blue Ridge, within walking distance. During the heyday of their production, lasting until the mid-1930s, it seemed as if everyone in Greenville worked there.

During this era of economic prosperity, Greenville became incorporated. An *Order Book* entry, dated November 24, 1884, described the request for government materials:

In the motion of William F. Smith, Mayor of the town of Greenville in this county, asking that he be supplied with the Session Acts, the Code of 1873 and Mayor's guide, it appearing to the court that said town of Greenville has been incorporated the last twelve months and that said corporation has never been supplied with such books once that no effort can be made for the same to any predecessor in office of said town, it is ordered to certified to the secretary of the Commonwealth that said Smith is entitled to said books provided it does not diminish the supply of the work so ipued below twenty-five copies.

Greenville's incorporation allowed its residents to elect its own officials and provided local control over what ordinances were passed and what taxes were collected. Burwell noted several years later in the May 15, 1888, issue of the *Argus* that the town was managing its affairs quite well: " . . . under an act of legislature their town was incorporated several years ago and the citizens have enjoyed the benefits of a good, healthy administration." A tongue-in-cheek comment followed later that year in the August 18th issue as follows:

Greenville certainly has a clever set of town fathers. Last year they did not assess a tax on the citizens, saying it was not necessary. Guess some of the grumblers of several years ago don't have so much to say about tax now.

Unfortunately, it was a lack of funds that contributed to the loss of Greenville's corporate status several years later.

Figure 30. Late nineteenth century Greenville.

21

Victorian Life

Greenville's renewed economic prosperity following the Civil War marked the beginning of the Victorian era. Improved communication via telegraph and railroad awakened Greenville to national trends in business, politics, and social life. Across the country, the work week was shortening, more money was available, and a new middle class of merchants and businessmen was emerging. As such, leisure time became fashionable and social activities captured the imagination of many townsfolk.

In contrast to the rather bleak early nineteenth century landscape, the Victorian era brought about a new interest in decorating both house and yard. One particular innovation became the rage — the large, spacious front porch. No longer was the porch, or the house-yard for that matter, viewed in merely functional terms. Rather, these spaces became outdoor rooms for socializing. With the increasing availability of pre-sawn woodwork, more and more houses could be updated with the addition of a porch adorned with decorative "gingerbread." It is not surprising that sitting out on the front porch to watch the traffic, talk with passerbys, and just enjoy the climate became a popular pastime.

Nevertheless, the social center of the community continued to be rooted in its churches. In its formative years, Bethel Church had served the majority of residents since nearly all were of Presbyterian, Scotch-Irish descent. As noted earlier, the Greenville Methodist Church was established in 1836,

159

although Brake has suggested that informal Methodist services were held in homes as early as 1800, before this congregation had organized. In addition, some traveled to St. Johns Evangelical and Reformed Church, established in the 1780s and located just past Bethel on the Howardsville Turnpike. Old Providence Church, too, was located only five miles to the southwest.

Between 1865 and 1890, several other churches had located in Greenville. Mount Ed Presbyterian Church was a small church located on Jack's Hill on the northwest border of town. This modest frame building was constructed soon after the Civil War and served the African-American community located on the northeast corner of town. It remained in regular use until the early 1960s; unfortunately, the building was razed in early 1993. A graveyard was located on the west edge of the churchyard; most of the markers are dated between 1900 and 1930, with the earliest reading 1893.

An African-American Methodist Church was located on an alley running between Main and Back streets on the south border of town. This church was also built after the War and is remembered by many today from when it was relocated along US Route 11 in the 1930s. This building was torn down in the 1980s.

Finally, the Greenville Baptist Church was built in 1884 for two-thousand dollars and was dedicated in the following year; there were only ten members in its congregation at the time. This large frame building was one of the first structures located on the hill west of town in New Greenville.

Revivals were extremely popular following the Civil War. Outside gatherings were a frequent occurrence, as congregations would crowd together under large tents to hear fervid testimonies and win new converts. The *Augusta County Argus* described one such event on December 14, 1887:

Protracted services are going on at the (Greenville) Methodist church, conducted by Rev. Wiley Smith, the evangelist, and they are attended every night by large and interested congregations. At this writing there have been three conversions - two at the altar.

The late Reverend Harry W. Craver provided the following anecdote regarding an incident that occurred at one of the revivals in Greenville.

> . . . *a great revival was held. Rev. Mr. Smith, the evangelist, was a powerful preacher and the community was stirred. Many joined the church and the church began to grow. During the meeting the evangelist prayed that a certain saloon was hindering the work of the Lord and on the next day the owner of the saloon was taken sick and later died. This incident made an impression upon many and it is retold even to this day.*

In addition to religious gatherings, nationally-organized social groups were the craze and proliferated across the country. In Greenville, many fraternities flourished, including the Freemasons, Oddfellows, and Young Mens' Christian Association (YMCA). Each of these organizations contributed to the Main Street landscape by building large, boastful meeting halls. The Freemasons erected one of the more dominant buildings on lot 2, north Main Street. The Masonic Hall was dedicated on February 15, 1886, replacing an older structure located just east of town; the Lodge had been chartered in Greenville since 1873. The new building presented a large facade with bold brackets supporting a heavy, projecting cornice. A small porch across the front, shading two large picture windows, marked the storefront for H. C. Clark's Mercantile on the first floor. The Masons met upstairs in a large hall and continue to hold monthly meetings there today.

The Oddfellows meeting hall was also built with a large decorative facade, but unlike the Masonic Hall was a long, narrow building occupying only a small portion of lot 10 next to the Steele House. The fraternity established its Greenville chapter in 1851 and the members built their hall at the turn of the century. Like the Masonic Lodge, this building was also adorned with bold brackets and cornice mouldings. It housed a pool hall and a barber shop in its early days followed by several grocery stores later on. The building was abandoned in the 1970s when the Oddfellows fraternity disbanded in Greenville. The Boy Scouts of America used the building for storage until it was razed.

The YMCA began meeting as early as 1888 in the old storehouse building located on lot 8, north Main Street, directly across from the Steele House. They met weekly on Sundays, and at one time claimed 175 members. Their building, one of the Greenville's oldest, had once served as the first Masonic lodge and was a blacksmith shop before that. Old timers remember its last use as Dorsey Vines' barber shop.

Another fraternity that was active throughout the 1870s and 1880s was the Veterans of the Fifth Virginia Regiment. There were many veterans from Greenville who met regularly and participated in larger Civil War reunions held throughout Virginia. The War had left many men physically disabled with as many more experiencing difficulty adjusting to civilian life; as such, reunion meetings were of great importance to these veterans all across Augusta County. In this regard, Jas. W. Newton, Major of the Fifth Regiment of Veterans wrote in the *Banner* (January 17, 1883) requesting community support as follows:

Many of the best soldiers we had — men who were always at the post of duty, who were foremost in the advance, and brought up the rear on a retreat, who sacrificed their all upon the altar of their country in those dark days of trial and danger, are to-day in moderate circumstances, and unless help is afforded them, they will be denied the pleasure of this trip, perhaps the greatest event of their lives. Citizens of Greenville, Middlebrook, West View, Fishersville, Mt. Solon, Sangersville, Spring Hill and their vicinities, I appeal to you to aid these men. Can't a festival, or oyster supper be given within the bounds of each company and the proceeds go to this object? Who will be the first lady to start the ball in motion? (referring to a reunion to be held at Niagara Falls on May 22, 1883)

In addition, the Confederate Veterans were honored each year in Augusta County as announced in the May 29, 1888, issue of the *Argus*, " . . . June 9, as is the date each year will be observed as Confederate Memorial Day. Persons in the County and City should see to the matter of having their lots in the cemetery in proper condition." This date not only coincided with the surrender of General Robert E. Lee's army at Appomattox, but also was the last date that General David Hunter occupied Staunton before moving his invading army south towards Lexington.

As part of the growing temperance movement across the country, Greenville supported its own Council of the Friends of Temperance (Chapter No. 62) following the Civil War. This group was active in a petition against licensing bars in Greenville in 1883. In this regard, an editorial in the *Banner* dated February 21, 1883, noted: "Some think two bars too many for Greenville, while Massie's Mill, Nelson County, a small place, has three." The petition was withdrawn several months later as reported on May 2, 1883: "We are not to have local option, and the Ginslinger is happy."

The temperance movement remained strong in Greenville. Numerous booklets, pamphlets, and flyers circulated throughout the county making impassioned pleas for total abstinence. Some told dire stories of God-fearing and devoted family men who, after taking a single innocent swallow of hard liquor, were destroyed by alcohol, becoming drunkards and allowing their neglected families to go into the poorhouse. This sentiment was reflected in a vignette provided by Reverend Craver:

> *Mr. Ballard Smith conducted a Tavern near the river as you come into Greenville. The passengers of the stage coach would stop for meals, drinks, or to spend the night. One night Mr. Smith went to the Methodist Church to hear a lecture on Temperance and so convinced of the cause of Temperance that he went to the tavern and threw all the whiskey into the nearby Middle [South] River and never served whiskey again.*

Men were not the only ones joining community organizations, as the women in Greenville also joined temperance and civic groups, meeting regularly to host social events and raise money for community projects. Oyster suppers were a popular fund raiser in the 1880s, usually held at one of the meeting halls. In fact, for several years, the Ladies of the Baptist Church hosted an oyster dinner and supper at the Masonic Hall on Thanksgiving Day.

Another popular event in Greenville was the spelling bee. Although the schools regularly held such contests for children, it was the adult competition that attracted large crowds from all the neighboring communities. Contestants had to be at least twenty-one years of age to compete and included schoolteachers, merchants, and whomever else prided themselves as a good speller. These events played to full houses, packing meeting halls, schoolrooms, and the parlors of Greenville. Apparently, the spelling bees could become quite spirited, as long-time resident Berl Steele remembered much cheering and sometimes arguing during a monthly competition in the 1920s.

During the summer months, well-publicized lawn parties were popular in Greenville. Visitors from all over southern Augusta County would come to feast and to compete in various contests and games. Berl and Edna Steele recalled a particular event called the "box party" during which young men would bid on the opportunity to share a box lunch with the local (and single!) girl who prepared it. A similar evening party at the Greenville Hotel was described in the *Argus* on July 24, 1888, as follows:

> An evening so full of enjoyment has seldom been spent by any of the young men so fortunate as to be present at the leap year party last Friday night, given by the young ladies of Greenville and vicinity at the hotel in Greenville. From the moment of their arrival until their departure, when day had embraced night and completely hid her from sight, for not one minute did the young ladies allow them to be deserted. Every possible attention was shown each and every young man and gave to them the justly earned credit of a greater success then they had ever made any party. The numerous blushes appearing on the faces of young men during apparently earnest conversation proved truly that the "old, old tale" was being poured into only too willing ears by sweet, fascinating and true women. Many, we learn, failing at first, proved at last the best motto is "Try, try again" by success with another. Everything conducive to joy, including an elegant repast served during the night, was looked after by the young ladies, and the minister present was only another example of their wise forethought. To attempt a description of the gentlemen or costumes would be worse than useless, so we will say that all looked neat and handsome and seemed doing their best to please. Many strangers were present and more pretty girls were never at any party than at this.

Greenville supported a baseball team, once called the "Greenville's Beanpoles" in the *Argus* (July 24, 1888), which played other local teams from Middlebrook, Stuarts Draft and Staunton. Berl Steele remembers the team forty years later as the "Greenville Scrubs" in the 1920s — named not for their skills a ballplayers, as they claimed many wins, but rather for their lack of uniforms. By this time, baseball games routinely drew crowds of over three-hundred in Greenville. The ball field was located behind the school house and adjoined the Hanger's backyard. A basketball team was also formed for both men and women in the mid-1920s.

On the more informal side, the game of horseshoes was very popular among the men of Greenville. Many such games took place in the early 1920s near the street corner on the edges of lots 7 and 8, south Main Street. Henry Apple was considered to be one of the best players at the time; he was also a master checker player and noted for his sense of humor, earning him the title of "Town Jester."

Across the street from the horseshoe stakes was the "Pop Shop," another favorite spot on Main Street in the 1920s. Berl Steele recalled that by 7:00 PM on Saturday all the farmers met in the store to discuss the events of the day. The new-fangled carbonated sodas were very popular among both adults and children, offering an appropriate substitute for alcoholic beverages to the temperance-minded. Initially, soda water was promoted for its medicinal properties, but the addition of flavored syrups made sodas extremely popular simply for their taste. Coca-cola was available by the 1890s and was very popular in Greenville, bringing five cents a glass.

Perhaps the biggest nightspot along the Main Street from the turn of the century up until the 1930s was Palmer's Store. Here large crowds gathered in the summer each weekend to hear the "barber shop quartet;" on any given night, there might be as many as seven or eight musicians singing and playing instruments on the front porch. Even the "barber shop" was a misnomer, as Palmers' Store was a general mercantile which sold nearly everything.

Finally, any discussion of Greenville's social life would be incomplete without mention of the peace-keeping activities of its officers. Greenville maintained a small jailhouse located along Back Street just behind the Masonic building. Established during the 1880s, it was used primarily as a holding cell for the drunk and disorderly before transporting them to Staunton. It was no longer used after 1914–1915 as related in the following story told by Berl Steele and paraphrased as follows:

Charles Shultz was the deputy at the time, and he was charged to deal with any disorderly conduct in Greenville. One night the two burly men had been hitting the liquor pretty hard and were getting loud and troublesome. Shultz locked them up in the jailhouse, but they became so restless, that they proceeded to tear the small building down from the inside out; no one dared to try and stop them. The jailhouse was never rebuilt.

One problem that Greenville had continual difficulty with was controlling the reckless riding of horses on the Main Street. In this regard, the July 7, 1882, editorial in the *Banner* read:

From the way some people ride along our main thoroughfare one might suppose they fancied themselves far out on the prairie with no obstructions within miles of them. We don't so much object to a moderate hard-gallop, but when it comes to dashing at break-neck speed it is entirely out of the question, endangering limb and life of persons who may be on the street, especially ladies and children.

In addition, the town had an annoying parking problem as evidenced by Burwell's lament that " . . . people who bring wagons here should not leave their teams standing on the streets in front of residences and in the way. This won't do gentlemen." Some things never change.

166

22

Black Greenville

A sizable African-American population had settled in Greenville by the end of the Civil War. In the early 1920s, there were forty or more African-American families living along Jack's Hill at the northwest corner of town. Twenty or more log houses of modest means lined the hill along the road leading to Staunton. They were built close together and were without wells, requiring the residents to climb down the bluffs to the river's edge to collect water and wash clothes.

Several of these log houses remain today, most notably the Fanny Thompson house located along the old Greenville Road (Virginia Route 1206) which runs atop the river bluffs. This structure was built during the second and third quarters of the nineteenth century. The log building was nearly square (16 by 17 feet) and contained a hall-and-parlor floorplan with a single, gable-end chimney. A two-bay fenestration with the doorway offset away from the chimney gable characterize the facade. The Fanny Thompson House had large lateral and second floor additions. Clapboarding once covered the logs but have since deteriorated from neglect. Inside, the detailing was simple with exposed floor joists and single bead moldings.

The Georgian and Victorian influences that characterize the homes of White residents are not evident in these modest houses. Rather, the older floorplans and fenestrations remained in use. This use of old designs is most likely attributable to the economic disadvantages suffered by the African-

Figure 31. Fanny Thompson House, circa 1865–1870. This log house along Jack's Hill is relatively unaltered since the cost of modernization was more than most African-American families could afford. In addition, the land was rocky and did not permit installation of plumbing; hence, few of these structures were chosen for renovation. As a result, the house represents one of the best examples of an original nineteenth-century dwelling located in Greenville; unfortunately, the building has decayed with neglect. The Fanny Thompson House narrowly escaped the rerouting of US Route 11 in the late 1930s, but the house has remained vacant for over twenty years and is currently in poor condition.

American population in Greenville; however, their houses serve as testimony to the durability of the old hall-and-parlor design.

This region along Jack's Hill was called "Black Greenville," or more pejoratively, "Nigger Town." Race relations were strained throughout the postwar period in Greenville. This tension was aptly described in an editorial published in the April 25, 1883, issue of the *Banner* as follows:

> *There are a number of colored idlers who almost every night have a dance on one or two porches in the central part of town where, to the music of the banjo, they kick up a great racket, and make the night hideous with*

168

their yells, all combining to annoy many of our people. Can our officers not sit down on and end this nuisance?

It is clear from the tone of Burwell's editorial that segregation was the norm. Into the 1920s, the African-American community was encouraged to reside and conduct their affairs north of the South River. In fact, no African-American man dared to cross the river bridge into town after dark without fear of being accosted.

Despite racial tensions, several African-American men gained respect for their skilled craftsmanship. The *Argus* reported on October 7, 1888: "Jas. Harrison, the old colored blacksmith at Greenville, exhibited at the fair a set of horseshoes, with the nails, which he made himself." Berl Steele remembered this man's reputation in the 1920s as the blacksmith who "could do anything."

23

More New Buildings

Throughout the Victorian era, many building improvements were made in Greenville as older buildings were radically modified or torn down and new ones built. The wide availability of pre-cut lumber and mass-produced wire nails gave rise to balloon framing; as in contemporary houses, lighter weight two-by-fours were used to frame-in floors, walls and roofs. This innovation allowed builders more flexibility in designing complex houses with multiple corners and irregular shapes; the rectangular block which characterized nearly all early houses was transformed into new shapes by adding false gables, bay windows, and multiple ells. Similarly, pre-cut gingerbread trim flooded the market, ushering in an era of home decorating; old and unfashionable houses could be made to look like new. The bulky and labor-intensive timber framing construction methods of the early to mid-nineteenth century became obsolete except in barns.

These technological advances broadened traditional conceptions of social status. Although high style brick houses remained a symbol of economic attainment, the wide assortment of house adornments, coupled with a burgeoning middle class that could afford them, redefined notions governing what contemporary and stylish houses should look like and made these ideals widely available. In short, the visual trappings of economic success could be bought and added to older and more modest houses. This social striving was further prompted by the publication of numerous deco-

171

rating guides and magazines.

It is not surprising that this synergism of technological and social influences marked the dawning of a building era that was unsurpassed in Greenville's history. New buildings of the latest style proliferated and old ones were remade in the Victorian mold; a mass-marketed "keeping up with the Joneses" began to take hold. Greenville developed a substantial skyline of large imposing buildings, each vying for a prominent place in the Main Street landscape: the Masons, the Oddfellows, the merchants. As such, Greenville was charging full steam ahead into the modern era and, like many small towns, was becoming a part of the national economy —

Figure 32. Main Street in Greenville, circa 1915. The juxtaposition of old and new upon a rapidly changing landscape is seen in this view of Main Street, looking north from the top of the hill. Both an automobile and a horse drawn carriage share parking space. The ornate cornice brackets of the Oddfellows Hall tower over the relatively sedate, unadorned lines of the Robert Steele House. The shake roof and overgrown front porch are symbolic of a bygone era and perhaps signal a stagnation or reluctance to embrace the new industrial age. The old two-story building located across the street once housed the YMCA and Masons; Roy Hanger's grocery store, with the small front porch, is located next to it. Most of the buildings shown here are now torn down.

particularly with the arrival of the railroads.

The result of Greenville's postwar building spurt is evident in the Main Street photograph taken around 1915 (see Figure 32). As the caption reveals, many of these buildings no longer stand. Of particular interest is the massive frame house located two lots down from the Steele House on lot 8 south Main Street. It was built right on the street like the Steele House, revealing the building's early date. It was a double house with the north portion being the oldest; it had a large gable chimney along the north wall. This may be the house built by Joseph Houston between 1818 and 1822 when he owned lots 8 through 10. The house was lifted from its foundation, turned ninety degrees and set back from the street sometime before 1920. It was used as a boarding home before being razed in 1929–1930.

Next to the old Huston place on lot 7, a new Greenville landmark was built: a gothic cottage named "Rosemont." Built by the prominent merchant R. H. Palmer, this house was once considered to be the finest in Greenville. Oral history passed down by Berl Steele suggested that R. H. Palmer personally supervised every step of its construction — he wanted it "just right."

The Gothic style was popularized by Andrew Jackson Downing's 1842 publication, a pattern book, entitled *Cottage Residences*. Rosemont was the town's first house built from a specific published model; as such, its design was less dependent upon the experiential building competence of local carpenters. The Gothic detailing was heavily influenced by the Old English cottages found in the British Isles; even the name Rosemont is evocative of the English gentry and reflects the continuing allure of the Old World order as the ideal model of economic success in the Valley. Palmer was, in effect, declaring his membership in the gentry class through association.

Rosemont was a single story high with twelve foot ceilings; tall windows trimmed with broad framing provided a balanced three bay facade with a prominent center gable. Large bay windows flanked the gable ends which were

Figure 33. Victorian houses in Greenville. Rosemont, circa 1880s, is pictured at the top. It is an ornate house with Gothic detailing influenced by the Victorian cottage movement, yet on the inside, the house is familiar with its central passageway floorplan flanked by three rooms on each side. The extravagant use of space (which includes high ceilings, a false gable, and a steep roof pitch without a second floor) underscores the importance given to fashion. The Spitler House, circa 1905, is pictured at the bottom soon after its construction. This house also displays decorative false gables and has a hipped roof, yet again, a very traditional, full Georgian floorplan is concealed inside. The modern name given to this house style is the "four-square." Of note, the two portions of the Samuel Finley House (divided in 1909) are shown next door.

decorated along the eaves with ornate vergeboards. In the rear, two parallel ells ran perpendicular to the main house, each containing two rooms — it was both a unique and very contemporary floorplan, yet not dissimilar to the first-floor full Georgian plan.

A second Victorian structure was built by J. E. Spitler directly across the alley from Rosemont in 1905. The lot had previously been the site of a large storehouse and a tavern, both serving patrons of the Greenville hotel located next door. The house that Spitler built was much larger than Rosemont but with less ornamentation; known as a "four-square" design, his house was a Georgian plan with a symmetrical facade and hipped roof. Center gables decorated with carved finials were located on each side and called attention to this high-style house. This house, too, was built from published plans.

Another major change in the Main Street landscape concerned the extensive alterations made to the "Antrium" or "Greenville Hotel" located on lots 4 and 5 on south Main Street. This hotel was originally the Samuel Finley House, circa 1797. J. H. Clarke, another prominent merchant whose dry-goods store was located in the Masonic building, had the hotel building cut into halves and moved back from the street to create two separate houses in 1909. Brake related that the late Earl Shultz described watching teams of mules pull the structure apart along large timber rails. Only the right half survives today, its original appearance modified by a two-story porch and a Victorian turret with gothic styling. These latter changes were completed for H. C. Minor who was a merchant in business with Clarke. As was the custom, he transformed this old building into a new one. The left half burned in the 1920s.

Yet another series of changes along the Main Street occurred when the Greenville Methodist congregation built a new church in 1899. The 1836 brick church was razed during the summer and a contemporary L-shaped, frame building was built for three-thousand dollars and dedicated on April 1, 1900. The original church bell was salvaged and continued to call people to worship for years to come. In December, 1908, tragedy struck just four days before Christmas, as the church caught fire that afternoon. The calamity was described in 1936 by the Reverend Harry W. Craver:

Rev. R. L. Eutsler says he had held services on Sunday, Dec. 20, 1908 at 11:00 A.M. and on his way to Mint Spring (about 2:00 P.M.) he received a phone call saying the church at Greenville was on fire. When he arrived in Greenville the roof had fallen in. The residence of Mrs. Phoepe Gentry, next to the church, was destroyed and the home of Wm. McGuffin was damaged by fire. The Staunton paper says "the community was aroused as it had not been aroused for many years". Two hundred persons formed a bucket brigade to feed the small hand pump which did a most effective piece of work and helped save the town. At one time more than 12 homes were on fire and a strong wind carried burning embers over the town. Through the Providence of God and the efforts of the people the town was saved.

The Greenville Baptist Church invited the congregation to worship there until a new sanctuary could be built. Unsolicited gifts for the new building began arriving the very next day; the present church was built during the following year with services resuming in January, 1910. The new building was constructed of cement to insure its longevity. It is decorated in the Victorian shingle style; large lancet arch stained glass windows are located along its walls with a similar motif defining the belfry. Sadly, the original church bell was lost to the fire. The new building is located over part of the church's cemetery; the earliest surviving gravestone is dated 1847.

In 1913, one of town's more enduring landmarks was constructed in the form of the Greenville School. The square, two-story brick edifice contained two classrooms on each floor with bathrooms on the first floor and a cafeteria on the second. The new schoolhouse replaced an aging single-story frame building located at the end of an alley running between lots 8 and 9 on south Main Street. The old school was housed in a long narrow building with a five-bay facade and four-columned portico marking the entrance; a stove in the central hallway provided heat. It had served the educational needs of the community since the 1890s when it had replaced an older three-room building.

Following the opening of the new school, the old building was moved from the west border of the school lot (to the right of the present school building) to the east side. There, the old school served as the Town Hall. In addition to Judical and Town Council meetings, the Hall provided space for a wide range of social events and extra classroom space during the academic year. The building was razed in the 1940s.

A second school building was added to the complex in 1927 which provided four more classrooms and a gymnasium in the basement. Berl and Edna Steele recall playing basketball on a hard dirt floor in 1928; Brake notes that chalk was secured from the local mines to mark out the playing court. The wood floor was completed the following year. Both school buildings were used until the opening of Riverheads High School in 1971.

While on schools, it is worth a digression to outline the various schools that were located in Greenville. One of the earliest references to a town school was in 1822; Drexel reported that this brick school building was built on Jack's Hill on the northwest border of town along the road leading to Staunton. A grammar school was later located in the Thomas Williams House in the 1860s. Several other private schools met for a time until a public grade school was opened in 1873. The 1884 Hotchkiss map located this schoolhouse on the western edge of the present school yard, behind lots 8 and 9 as mentioned above. Also shown on this map, an African-American school was located along the Valley Pike just south of town.

This period of postwar prosperity was reflected in several improvements to the Steele House. Already mentioned was the Victorian porch added around 1885, which, when viewed in the context of the changes going on in Greenville, was in keeping with the town's overall transformation. The porch is full length, effectively de-emphasizing the old brick by projecting the fresh, modern look of delicately-shaped newels, pickets, and railings. Despite being distracted by his mountain retreat, Lewis McGilvray took the time to embrace the emerging Victorian fashion.

When Roy and Olivia Hanger took residence there in 1902, several renovations were made to the interior of the house, including replastering damaged wall areas and modifying the stairwell to broaden it and provide a small landing in the central hall. The plaster walls were covered with a heavily patterned paper and bright linoleum was laid on the floor in every room. With the invention of the spiral spring for furniture, upholstered chairs and couches were becoming the rage — gone was the hardwood furniture of the antebellum days.

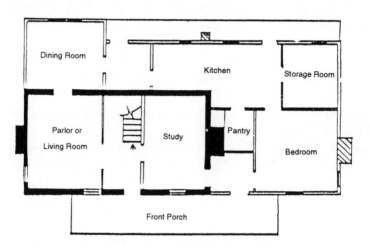

Figure 34. Rear additions to the Robert Steele House, 1902. Roy and Olivia Hanger closed-in the back porch and built additional rooms along the rear of the house to provide kitchen, pantry, and storage rooms. The trend which started with the detached kitchen was continued: the service rooms were pushed towards the back of the house and away from the formal spaces. The lateral addition housed a third bedroom (remember that two bedrooms were located upstairs), and the back left corner became the dining room when the front room located to the right of the central passageway was used as a study. The front room to the left of the central passageway was used as a parlor or living room. The unlabeled rooms in the floorplan pictured above served as passageways, foyers, and storage rooms. On balance, the house continued to evolve with the needs of its owners reflecting new patterns of domestic and social life.

178

A second frame addition, running laterally across the rear of the house, was added to provide kitchen and service rooms. As such, domestic activities were pushed further to the back of the house, freeing the front rooms for social activities. Even the rear doorway from the dining room (the hall) was plastered over to limit intrusions upon the formal spaces. Just as Greenville was enjoying a thorough cosmetic makeover in anticipation of the twentieth century, so too was the Steele House experiencing changes that would extend its life into the new era.

24

More Psychological Influences

Spurred on by the industrial revolution, the railroads, and technological advances in communication, a consumer-oriented economy emerged throughout the eastern United States during the period between 1880 and 1920. Purchasing power had never been greater in the Valley, and the range of available goods was extensive. The building spurt in Greenville at the turn of the century was as much a product of these economic factors as well as deeper psychological strivings.

Just as the building of center-hall I-houses went beyond fashion in bringing its owner a sense of personal satisfaction and esteem, so too did the purchasing of the latest products. American ingenuity hit a high point — new technologies were revolutionizing farming, business, transportation, and communication. Advances in home construction coupled with a burgeoning home improvement industry prompted a rapid and near complete transformation of the architectural landscape; with few exceptions, every house in Greenville was updated with Victorian details, modern tin roofs, and newly landscaped yards.

The expanding economy contributed to a national consciousness; a common American experience was emerging. It was promoted in the advertising media, it was shaped by the products people bought, and it was taught to children in schools. On a more material level, the railroad allowed Greenville residents to enjoy the same products enjoyed by residents of New York City.

Small towns like Greenville could gain distinction on economic terms; it comes as no surprise that Greenville became incorporated in 1883 (some 89 years after the first lots were sold along the Main Street). Incorporation meant economic autonomy. Greenville sought to compete directly with rival marketplaces, including Staunton and Waynesboro. On a psychological level, Greenville had attained a renewed respectability — the town was a bona fide part of the national economy.

Whereas the early Valley settlers sought refuge in their Old World traditions when confronted with the challenges of the frontier, their descendants in the early twentieth century were ready to abandon the old ways to become part of the national scene. Progress was fashionable. To own the latest automobile, kitchen appliance, or farm implement was synonymous with social status. Alternatively, to be without the newest items was to be "backwards" and "behind the times."

The psychology behind this new American ethic was a deeply complicated one which goes beyond the scope of this book; yet, it was not unlike the sentiments we experience today when automakers and fast food vendors champion patriotic themes as part of their advertising efforts. "Buy American," "Take pride in your neighborhood," "American ingenuity" — these were the rallying cries of a national economy. Such slogans tapped into people's self-esteem and patriotism; they created a huge demand for the products of a burgeoning industrial society.

Together, all these influences — psychological and economic — spelled the end of the vernacular architectural tradition in Greenville. Despite the near-domination of the Georgian ideal throughout the nineteenth century, the industrial era ushered in the advent of the national house design. Local building traditions began to fade, as published house plans and blue-prints became widely available. The Victorian cottage named Rosemont is perhaps one of the earliest national house types built along Greenville's Main Street; it was a novel design with few local predecessors, yet similar cottages were appearing all over America at about the same time. Its design tells more about national architectural trends than it does about those in the Valley.

Rosemont was not conservative in its styling; therefore, it was not copied in Greenville. In contrast, a number of more conservative national house types did become popular. Several bungalow and four-square house designs were built along the Main Street in the 1920s. These were simple houses with few ornaments. As testimony to the conservative climate of the upper Valley, and perhaps as a backlash to the initial excesses of the Victorian era, white paint became the standard for residential buildings. For a while, all of Greenville, and much of the Valley, was painted white.

25

Decline

The experiences shared by Roy and Olivia Hanger over the years reflected the changing fortunes of Greenville as it evolved from a thriving rural marketplace and community to a sleepy, bedroom community dependent upon Staunton and Waynesboro for economic support. Theirs was not a sad story unique to Greenville; rather, it highlighted a trend felt throughout the Valley — a trend towards urbanization and centralization of the economy.

Roy Hanger owned and operated a small grocery store and butcher's shop. A slaughter house was built behind the house next to the school yard. Since money was tight for the Hanger's, his extended family helped him build a storehouse across the street on the edge of lot 9. Berl Steele fondly remembers stopping by the shop after school and watching with amazement as Roy deftly carved the meats.

His business was prosperous despite the presence of three other grocery stores in Greenville at the time. Unfortunately, merchants like Hanger were increasingly unable to compete with the larger stores located in Staunton and Waynesboro which stocked more goods at lower prices. One general store that did survive was the business started by J. E. Spitler at the turn of the century. The store was later operated by his son, Howe Spitler, until his death in July, 1980; at that time, it was the longest running family grocery business in Augusta County.

One of the chief factors responsible for this economic

decline was the advent of the automobile. Cars were considered somewhat of a novelty until Henry Ford's assembly lines brought them within the financial reach of the middle class. By 1916, a shiny black Ford Model T could be had for under four-hundred dollars. A photograph published by Brake suggests that these horseless carriages rumbled through Greenville as early as 1910; however, the first motor vehicle owned by a Greenville resident was Wilber Palmer's Model T pickup truck. This truck immediately replaced Palmer's wagons for hauling goods to and from his store. Soon after, a second motor vehicle was purchased by rival store proprietor John H. Clarke.

In the early 1920s, an automobile dealership was established in a large concrete block building located on lot 9 south Main Street next to the Oddfellows Hall; Star and Durant automobiles were sold here. This showroom remained in

Figure 35. South Main Street in Greenville, early 1930s. The Eastern Standard Oil Company ushers in a new era which contrasts sharply with the small freight wagon of days not so distant. Note the glass-top gasoline pumps dating back to the mid-1920s. The Greenville Methodist Church stands on the knoll to the right.

business for about ten years when it was replaced by an apple packing plant. The first gas pumps were at the Esso station located on the Valley Pike at the southern border of town. By the mid-1930s there were three service stations in Greenville.

Directly related to increasing motor traffic was the widescale resurfacing and rerouting of roads. No other improvement more dramatically altered the Greenville landscape of this era than the shifting of US Route 11 to run along Back Street. The surveying of the new route was completed in 1933 and shortly thereafter Back Street was regraded, cutting a deep path through the top of the hill, and connected to US Route 11 at either end of town. Main Street was completely bypassed. Three or four dwellings were razed during the road building, and both the old Esso station and the African-American Methodist Church were relocated on the west side of the new road.

As automobiles became common in the 1930s, more and more people traveled to larger cities to shop. Country site-seeing jaunts became a Sunday afternoon obsession. Consequently, both economic and social pursuits took people away from Greenville. Local merchants slowly began to disappear, many of them relocating to Staunton. Roy Hanger eventually closed his business; he and Olivia worked for the postal service for many years in Greenville.

Throughout the Victorian era technical innovations were bringing the townfolks closer to the outside world. The first telephone line was connected to Palmer's store in the late 1890s and was advertised at five cents a call. Prior to that time electronic communication was limited to the telegraph office at the B&O Railroad depot on the west side of town. Brake noted that the public had so enjoyed the telegraph that private lines were hooked-up between some residences for entertainment.

Perhaps the most influential advancement in linking Greenville to the rest of the world was the radio. One of the first radios was owned by Ellis Mitchell who lived in the house on lot 8, north Main Street. Social events were increasingly shaped by radio and television; in this regard, Berl

Steele recalled the days when all the local men sat on the floor in the parlor of this house to listen to the 1924 World Series; this was when Washington barely edged past New York, four games to three.

Another innovation was the indoor bathroom. The first one in Greenville was located in the Palmer House. Since public water was not available until the late 1980s, many homes in Greenville remained without indoor plumbing until that time. Water, however, was easily acquired by a combination of rain-collecting cisterns and wells, although most families living in Black Greenville still had to make daily trips to the river to fetch water and wash clothes.

In contrast to the rapid changes taking place during the first quarter of the twentieth century, Dr. Hansford Thomas, Jr., related a series of events that were instrumental in slowing Greenville's initiation into the wider technological world. A Civic Club was organized in October, 1945, to address the needs of the town; however, club participation and interest waned, and little was accomplished. When the issue of bringing natural gas lines into town to provide modern lighting was broached by the club, the prevailing sentiment was shaped by fears about ruptured lines and fuel fires. As a result, the citizenry refused to allow the gas lines to be brought into town, whereas other towns like Stuarts Draft, considerably smaller than Greenville at the time, warmly embraced the idea. This conservatism also delayed the arrival of electricity as well. Greenville was left in the dark until power lines were erected in the 1920s.

A blow to the town's economic status occurred around the turn of the century when torrential rains caused the mill dam to overflow, washing out the US Route 11 bridge. The town coffers were empty and the council had to renounce its corporate status so the county could take responsibility for repairing the bridge.

Another pivotal event which altered the economic course of Greenville occurred in 1928. The DuPont Corporation tried to purchase the Smith Tavern Property bordering the South River. The farm contained several hundred acres at the time and was viewed as a good site for a factory. The Smith family refused to sell; DuPont moved its interest to Waynesboro where it located a large industrial complex along the South River.

Perhaps more symbolic than anything else was the closing of Greenville's only bank. The Bank of Riverheads, started in 1905, closed its doors forever in January, 1931, amidst the Great Depression. The building stood vacant for many years afterwards while bank buildings proliferated in Staunton.

As Greenville began to lose its social and economic identity, the town also began to lose its families; younger residents typically moved away to start new lives. When Roy Hanger passed away in 1959, following the death of Olivia Hanger two years earlier, the house fell into disrepair and remained vacant for over ten years. In 1968, a chancery court settled the estate among three surviving daughters: Margaret, Lucille, and Blanche. Descriptions of the house revealed the general lack of modernization completed over the years the Hangers owned it.

In a deposition taken in September, 1968, the house was described as "in rather poor condition" noting further "to repair this house would be prohibitive." The house had no bathroom or plumbing except a hand pump and sink in the kitchen connected to a cistern located on the north side. The house and lot were appraised at $3750 and were purchased at this price by Earle and Bessie Shultz in 1968.

In 1978, the VHLC designated the house as the McGilvray-Hanger House, as these two families had been prominent in its 165 year history; together, these families owned the property 105 years. The house was not alone in its dilapidation, as Main Street was filled with sagging structures in need of paint and repair. Throughout the 1970s and 1980s many of the old and long-vacant buildings were torn down, but unlike previous times, new construction did not take their place. Berl Steele mentioned that several old-timers who returned to visit Greenville had to be *convinced* that this was the town of their youth — it looked so different: lots that had two or three buildings squeezed onto them were now vacant and overgrown with weeds. On the other hand, newcomers were surprised to learn that this village was once a crowded marketplace.

26

Revitalization

Greenville celebrated its bicentennial in 1994, providing the opportunity for the town's many new residents to discover its past. For some, Greenville represents a rural retreat from urban life. For others, it is a return to small town living where neighbors know one another. For still others, the town provides affordable living. And finally, some were drawn by the allure of history. They join the residents who have lived in Greenville for most of their lifetimes, bearing witness to the many changes which have shaped Greenville's evolution into a quiet residential community.

The slow but steady growth of Augusta County, Staunton, and Waynesboro in the past decade (the population increased 7.4% between 1980 and 1990) has benefitted Greenville in several ways. Rural roads have been improved, prompting the spread of residential development into the far reaches of Augusta County. Towns located along US Route 11 have become increasingly popular as real estate continues to be bargain-priced compared to the Staunton and Waynesboro markets. The commute into the cities is an easy one, particularly since the advent of Interstate 81 in 1978. More and more people are moving to the countryside.

With so many people building homes in rural southern Augusta County, the need for convenience stores has lead to the resurrection of the old country store. Selling a little bit of everything from medicinal items and groceries to hardware and hunting/fishing gear — not to mention video rentals —

nearly every small village including Greenville, Steeles Tavern, Middlebrook, and Mint Spring, has one. Several of these general stores have become social centers where locals gather around a snackbar counter and talk about the news just like the old-timers did in Palmer's and Clark's stores.

Early in its most recent revitalization, the willingness of people to live outside the cities to decrease the cost of housing prompted many landowners to renovate the houses along Greenville's Main Street for use as rental properties. Many of the older houses were saved by this demand. This opportunity has not been lost on developers either, as much of the countryside surrounding Greenville has been subdivided into residential lots, including Indian Ridge just north of town and Spitler's Farm at the foot of Staley's Hill; these properties have sold briskly. In the wake of these developments, Greenville began to attract potential homebuyers willing to renovate individual residences. Since 1990, these efforts have been directed at the Smith Tavern, Breckenridge-Vines House, Valley Bank building, Palmer Store, Mitchell House, and the Steele House.

These renovations mark the latest of the town's many building periods. Yet, unlike the periods of growth experienced in the 1790s, 1830s, and 1880s, the current era is not one of new construction. Rather, the improvements have involved the updating of electrical and plumbing systems as well as the widespread use of maintenance-free building materials on existing houses. County water became available in 1989, reducing reliance upon cisterns, wells, and springs. But most noticeable has been the disappearance of chipped and weather-faded clapboards under aluminum or vinyl siding. Not only has this innovation caused houses to appear more uniform, but it also has introduced a wider range of colors to the heretofore all-white Main Street landscape.

As the traffic along US Route 11 increases, Greenville once again shows signs of considerable economic development. Two grocery stores, a specialty cheese shop, a bank, and two antique shops have been established in town; in addition, several restaurants and gas stations have been located by the

Interstate 81 exit a mile north of town.

The building of a ball field in Greenville by the local Ruritan organization in the 1980s has had a major impact upon the community. Not since the 1930s has the cheering of crowds and the smell of concession foods filled the air in Greenville. The field has also been the site of an annual carnival and parade down Main Street for the past several years. Symbolic of Greenville's steady revitalization, the parade was no small affair, as it was the first time in nearly half a century that the residents of the town gathered along Main Street to watch a parade! "It's about time someone woke this town up," a long-time Greenville resident exclaimed. The September 6, 1992, edition of the *Staunton News Leader* described the event as follows:

> *... families headed out to their front yards with lawn chairs while others chose a local store porch or lined U.S. 11 to get a good view. A Civil War re-enactment group fired a show round while a mountain man, in full fur regalia, later followed suit. Fire engines sounded sirens while antique and classic vehicles cruised by in showy silence. A clown walking her invisible dog hammed it up while a tiny beauty queen waved demurely.*

Amidst Greenville's resurgence came a challenge from the Augusta County Board of Supervisors that threatened to steal away part of the town's heritage. In anticipation of the Emergency 911 phone system, all the roads in the county were assigned names during the summer of 1992. The name chosen for Greenville's Main Street was Back Street! Apparently, the confusion began when US Route 11 was rerouted along the original Back Street thereby making it part of the Lee-Jackson Highway. Then, in 1947, the Virginia Department of Taxation created tax maps for the county which inadvertently labeled the Main Street as Back Street, presumably because the street had been bypassed and was no longer part of the main highway. This error remained until the E–911 program brought it to the public's attention.

Greenville residents were in an uproar. The August 2, 1992, edition of the *News Leader* reported the following reactions:

Velma Thorne, born on Main Street and at 85 its oldest resident, persuasively lobbied Riverheads Supervisor J. Donald Hanger. "I told him: You can't take us off of Main Street. I was here before you was born," she recounted.

In a rare community effort, sixteen residents of Greenville's Main Street appealed to the County Board of Supervisors during a public hearing. Brake and others brought deeds and maps to defend the argument that the town be allowed to keep its Main Street. The verdict was reported in the *News Leader* as follows:

Because the county has seven or more main streets, county officials originally decided to change all of them. However, supervisors relented last week when impassioned Greenville residents asked that Back Street be changed back to its original name, Main Street.

Consequently, Greenville earned the distinction of being the only town in Augusta County with a Main Street. Some controversy continued, however, as other towns realized that they had missed their opportunity to lobby for a Main Street of their own. An editorial in the August 5, 1992, edition of the *News Leader* made this observation:

Why all the fuss about having only one Main Street, putting it in Greenville, and getting rid of the one in Stuarts Draft? Though there can't be any duplication of street names because of the E-911 system, you could just use "alternate" spellings: Mane Street, Maine Street and so on.

With its tradition preserved, its residents finding issues and events to unite them, Greenville continues . . .

Epilogue

I have provided but a glimpse of the cultural and economic development of a small village in western Virginia. There is much more history here than we can ever hope to know. By examining the evolution of the Robert Steele House, my endeavor to know about my house became a study of human intentions, a saga of pioneers on the Virginia frontier defining their surroundings.

These pioneers left few records about how it was to live here, but their houses remain, revealing their day-to-day patterns of living, their yearnings to become "respectable," and their shaping of intimate living spaces. The buildings they crafted represented tangible creations which defined a new American ethic. This is the story that a history of Greenville has to tell: how a ford in the South River, situated along an old Indian path, became a prosperous rural market-place, with a pattern of growth and decline common to many small communities in the Valley.

The architectural record reveals the many ups and downs experienced by the residents of Greenville over the past 200 years — excited building spurts punctuated by periods of relative calm and occasional depression. Yet people continued to thrive here. This town was the New World for the Beards, Doaks, Hawpes, Jacksons, Mitchells, Steeles, and Tates, among many others. As the original trustees had predicted in December, 1793, Greenville became a place of "considerable commerce and traffic," but more importantly, Greenville

195

Figure 36. Renovations to the Second Smith Tavern. The brick facade which was added in 1953 was removed in 1996 revealing the original log structure. Evidence of an early doorway can be seen under the first floor window in the center of the log structure. The logs are in very good condition and have probably been covered since the early 1800s.

became a place of "particular advantages."

The striving to make Greenville significant and to be a part of this process is a theme that underlies all the events told here. This drive was not satisfied by the early economic successes of the 1830s, nor was it dampened by the tragedy of Civil War. It did not give way when steam locomotives introduced Greenville to the national economy. No, the striving of its residents to make Greenville a place of particular advantages was personal; it was part of the uniquely human search for meaning.

This sentiment is as much a part of Greenville today as it is in any village, town, or city. For some, it is revealed in a quest for history. As Greenville's local historian, John Brake once described:

You go down to the courthouse and there's no mention of Greenville, *the head of the headwaters of the South River in Augusta County. The more I read, I began to say, "Why is Greenville being ignored?" I said, "I've got to do something about this and see what's going on; I want to show them what really came out of Greenville." (*Staunton News Leader; *October 15, 1991)*

This sentiment reflects Greenville's heritage. To walk the Main Street and view the clapboarded log houses, the brick Georgian dwellings, and the ornate Victorian cottages is to directly experience the impact of this heritage.

Robert Steele had his house built such that it proclaimed his stature, and he chose to build it in Greenville. Perhaps this is why the house had such an impact upon me when I first saw it. Behind its plain and unpretentious facade, I sensed a deeper significance. This is why I was compelled to take this journey in the first place.

References

Augusta County Court Records.

Brake, J. (1981). Greenville, Virginia. *Augusta Historical Bulletin*, 17(2), 32–47.

Brake, J. (1986). *The Greenville United Methodist Church: 150th Anniversary, 1836–1986*. Greenville, VA: Greenville United Methodist Church.

Brice, M. M. (1965). *Conquest of a Valley*. Charlottesville, VA: University Press of Virginia.

Chappell, E. A. (1977). *Cultural Change in the Shenandoah Valley: Northern Augusta County Houses Before 1861*. Charlottesville, VA: Master's thesis, School of Architecture, University of Virginia.

Chappell, E. A. (1980). Acculturation in the Shenandoah Valley: Rhenish Houses of the Massanutten Settlement. *Proceedings of the American Philosophical Society*, 124(1), 55–89.

Church, B. H. (1978). *The Early Architecture of the Lower Valley of Virginia*. Charlottesville, VA: Master's thesis, School of Architecture, University of Virginia.

Couper, W. (1952). *History of the Shenandoah Valley*. New York, NY: Lewis Historical Publishing Co.

Drexel, N. D. (1940). Greenville, a historic town of Augusta. *Staunton News Leader*.

Driver, R. J. (1986). *52nd Virginia Infantry*. Lynchburg, VA: H. E. Howard.

Glassie, H. (1975). *Folk Housing in Middle Virginia*. Knoxville, TN: University of Tennessee Press.

Glassie, H. (1972). *Eighteenth-Century Cultural Process in Delaware Valley Folk Building*. Winterthur Portfolio, 7, 29–57.

Hamrick, R. M. Jr. (1982). Mills and Milling in Augusta County. *Augusta Historical Bulletin*, 18(2), 4–18.

Hawke, D. F. (1988). *Everyday Life in Early America*. New York, NY: Harper & Row.

Hotchkiss, J., and J. A. Waddell. (1885). *Historical Atlas of Augusta County, Virginia*. Chicago, IL: Waterman & Watkins.

Hubka, T. (1979). Just Folks Designing: Vernacular Designers and the Generation of Form. *Journal of Architectural Education*, 32(3), 27–29.

Jenkins, M. (1967). Ground Rules of Welsh Houses: A Primary Analysis. *Folk Life*, 5, 65–91.

Kercheval, S. (1925). *A History of the Valley of Virginia*. Strausburg, VA: Shenandoah Publishing House.

Kirkpatrick, D., and E. C. Kirkpatrick. (1985). *Rockbridge County Marriages, 1778–1850*. San Bernardino, CA: Borge Press.

Kniffen, F. (1965). Folk Housing: A Key to Diffusion. *Annals of the Association of American Geographers*, 55(4), 549–77.

Kniffen, F., and H. Glassie. (1966). Building in Wood in the Eastern United States: A Time-place Perspective. *Geographical Review*, 56(1), 40–66.

Larkin, J. (1988). *The Reshaping of Everyday Life: 1790–1840*. New York, NY: Harper & Row.

Lay, E. K., and N. M. Pawlett. (1981). Architectural Surveys Associated with Early Road Systems. *Association for Preservation Technology Bulletin*, 12(2), 3–20.

Leyburn, J. G. (1962). *The Scotch-Irish: A Social History*. Chapel Hill, NC: University of North Carolina Press.

Loth, C. (1974). Notes on the Evolution of Virginia Brickwork from the Seventeenth Century to the Late Nineteenth Century. *Association for Preservation Technology Bulletin*, 6(2), 82–120.

MacMaster, R. K. (1988). *Augusta County History: 1865–1950*. Staunton, VA: Augusta County Historical Society.

MacMaster, R. K. (1980). Captain James Patton Comes to America, 1737–1740. *Augusta Historical Bulletin*, 16(2), 4–13.

McAlester, V., and L. McAlester. (1991). *A Field Guide to American Houses*. New York, NY: Alfred A. Knopf.

McCleary, A. (1983). Old Homes of Augusta County: A Survey. *Augusta Historical Bulletin*, 19(1), 4–21.

McGinnis, C. (1993). *Virginia Genealogy: Sources and Resources.* Baltimore, MD: Genealogical Publishing Co.

Mitchell, R. D. (1977). *Commercialism and Frontier: Perspectives on the Early Shenandoah Valley.* Charlottesville, VA: University Press of Virginia.

Patterson, C. G. (1985). Stuart's Draft, Virginia. *Augusta Historical Bulletin,* 20(2), 57–62.

Peyton, J. L. (1985/1882). *History of Augusta County, Virginia.* Harrisonburg, VA: C. R. Carrier Co.

Robinson, D. G. (1977). *The Academies of Virginia: 1776–1861.* USA: D. G. Robinson.

Rouse, P. (1973). *The Great Wagon Road from Philadelphia to the South.* New York, NY: McGraw-Hill.

Schlereth, T. J. (1991). *Victorian America: Transformations in Everyday Life.* New York, NY: Harper-Collins Inc.

Scholfield, P. H. (1958). *The Theory of Proportion in Architecture.* Cambridge, Great Britain: Syndics of the Cambridge University Press.

Schouler, J. (1990/1906). *Americans of 1776: Daily Life in Revolutionary America.* Bowie, MD: Heritage Books.

Short, J. (1864). Handwritten letter dated June 6, 1864 from private collection.

Simpson, P. H. (1980). The Molded Brick Cornice in the Valley of Virginia. *Association for Preservation Technology Bulletin,* 12(4), 29–33.

Sloane, E. (1974). *Our Vanishing Landscape.* New York, NY: Ballantine Books.

Steinitz, M. (1989). Rethinking Geographical Approaches to the Common House: The Evidence from Eighteenth-century Massachusetts. In T. Carter, and B. L. Herman (eds.), *Perspectives in Vernacular Architecture,* III (16–26). Columbia, MO: University of Missouri Press.

Sutherland, D. E. (1989). *The Expansion of Everyday Life: 1860–1876.* New York, NY: Harper & Row.

Turner, H. S., and J. Sprout. (1974). *Bethel and Her Ministers, 1746–1946* (2nd ed.). Verona, VA: McClure Press.

Touart, P. B. (1986). The Acculturation of German-American Building Practices of Davidson County, North Carolina. In C. Wells (ed.), *Perspectives in Vernacular Architecture,* II (72–80). Columbia, MO: University of Missouri Press.

Townsend, A. A., and J. Cornman. (1884). *Representative Enterprises, Manufacturing and Commercial of the South and Southwest. The Valley of Virginia; Its Unequaled Resources. Staunton, VA.; A Sketch of the City, Her Live Business Houses and Educational and Charitable Institutions.* Staunton, VA: Valley Virginian Power Press.

Waddell, J. A. (1986/1886). *Annals of Augusta County, Virginia, from 1726 to 1871.* Harrisonburg, VA: C. J. Carrier Co.

Wallace, L. A. (1988). *5th Virginia Infantry.* Lynchburg, VA: H. E. Howard.

Wayland, J. W. (1964). *The German Element of the Valley of Virginia.* Bridgewater, VA: C. J. Carrier Co.

Wayland, J. W. (1976). *Twenty-five Chapters on the Shenandoah Valley* (2nd ed.). Harrisonburg, VA: C. J. Carrier Co.

Weaver, D. L. (1987). *Here Lyeth.* Greenville, VA: D. L. Weaver.

Wells, C. (1986). Old Claims and New Demands: Vernacular Architecture Studies Today. In C. Wells (ed.), *Perspectives in Vernacular Architecture,* II (1–10). Columbia, MO: University of Missouri Press.

Wenger, M. (1986). The Central Passage in Virginia: Evolution of an Eighteenth-century Living Space. In C. Wells (ed.), *Perspectives in Vernacular Architecture,* II (137–149). Columbia, MO: University of Missouri Press.

Wenger, M. (1989). The Dining Room in Early Virginia. In T. Carter, and B. L. Herman (eds.), *Perspectives in Vernacular Architecture,* III (149–159). Columbia, MO: University of Missouri Press.

Wolf, S. G. (1993). *As Various as Their Land: The Everyday Lives of Eighteenth Century Americans.* New York, NY: Harper-Collins.

Woods, E. (1972). *Albemarle County in Virginia.* Harrisonburg, VA: C. J. Carrier Co.

Wust, K. (1969). *The Virginia Germans.* Charlottesville, VA: University Press of Virginia.

Upton, D. (1982). *Vernacular Domestic Architecture in Eighteenth-century Virginia.* Winterthur Portfolio, 17(2–3), 95–119.

Upton, D., and J. M. Vlach. (1986). Introduction. In D. Upton and J. M. Vlach (eds.), *Common Places: Readings in American Vernacular Architecture* (xiii–xxiii). Athens, GA: University of Georgia Press.

Vogt, J., and T. W. Kethley. (1986). *Augusta County Marriages, 1748–1850.* Athens, GA: Berian Publishing Co.

202

Index